BRETT —

YOU ARE AN
AMAZING PERSUADOR !

Your Friend

Subliminal
Persuasion

INFLUENCE &
MARKETING
SECRETS
THEY DON'T
WANT YOU TO KNOW

DAVE LAKHANI

WILEY

John Wiley & Sons, Inc.

Published by John Wiley & Sons, Inc., Hoboken, New Jersey.
Published simultaneously in Canada.

For general information on our other products and services or for technical support, please contact our Customer Care Department within the United States at (800) 762-2974, outside the United States at (317) 572-3993, or fax (317) 572-4002.

Wiley also publishes its books in a variety of electronic formats. Some content that appears in print may not be available in electronic books. For more information about Wiley products, visit our web site at www.wiley.com.

Library of Congress Cataloging-in-Publication Data:

Lakhani, Dave, 1965–
    Subliminal persuasion : influence & marketing secrets they don't want you to know / Dave Lakhani.
        p. cm.
    Includes bibliographical references and index.
    ISBN 978-0-470-24336-7 (cloth/cd-rom)
        1. Subliminal advertising.   2. Subliminal projection.   3. Marketing—Psychological aspects.   I. Title.
    HF5827.9.L35   2008
    658.8001'9—dc22

                                                                2007041571

Printed in the United States of America.

10 9 8 7 6 5 4 3 2 1

This book is dedicated
with love to Stephanie and Austria
and
To the memory of
Mabel McKelroy and Nina Houston

CONTENTS

FOREWORD

I confess that I read things, see life, and business, a lot differently than most people do.

For me, people in sales and marketing are heroes. Without them there is no company, no hiring of Uncle Joe to work in Engineering, the Lab, the Front Office.

"If I can persuade, I can move the universe," said Frederick Douglas. (Douglas was a black slave who escaped to freedom in the 1850's and became a well known abolitionist and orator.)

People who can't persuade are impotent. . . .

Persuasion is the purpose and intention of communication. You tell your spouse, "my, you look gorgeous . . ."

Why?

You have an intention.

Are you simply broadcasting the news to her? . . . Newsflash, Jane looks absolutely smashing, film at 11.

No.

You are communicating a message to her that has at least two purposes. Sharing a fact with her, and, persuading her of that fact, and perhaps there are other reasons as well.

"Eat your food, young man." My Mom, never gave up on getting me to eat vegetables. She was persuasive and had multiple intentions.

She wanted me to eat so I wouldn't be hungry, she wanted me healthy for lots of reasons, she wanted me to have a better life.

"Honey the dog is outside."

Another newsflash?

Of course not. It's a message of multiple intentions most of which are persuasive the least being, "hey at least I put the dog out," or perhaps, "see I do pitch in, I put the dog out," or perhaps, "I put the dog out, let her in later on because I'm off to bed."

"I love you."

Certainly that isn't a persuasive message . . .

. . . but it is. One of the most intentional persuasive messages there is.

It might mean, "you are great and mean the world to me and please know that," where you are trying to create a bridge from your feelings to hers."

It could mean something in the future. She doesn't know you broke her necklace and when you tell her tomorrow, you'd like her to have built up a set of messages that create an image so she doesn't take your life when you tell her what happened.

Or it might mean, "let's go to bed," or, "I appreciate you," again with the purpose of creating an image of you in addition to sending a message of appreciation.

This isn't to say that all communication is intentionally designed to persuade other people to your way of thinking. That is simply not the case.

Life would be much easier if people would communicate with the intention to persuade. Most people simply communicate without thought or plan and then that message, however it is received becomes persuasive for something, about something, in the person's mind.

It's extremely hard to create a message with or without intention that doesn't persuade.

"It's 78 degrees outside."

Oh my, the weatherman says it will be a nice day, I won't need a jacket.

The weatherman said it was 78 degrees. You made up the rest. But it was a persuasive message because it got you to change your behavior. The weatherman personally might not care what you wear to work. He might have simply been "reading the weather" to get paid. But his message still persuaded.

"Dear God, Please let Daddy get a new heart. I really love him a lot."

We attempt to persuade God. In fact a lot of people attempt to persuade and negotiate with God asking for more and offering less than in any other negotiations they enter into.

In the Bible Abraham bargained for the Cities of Sodom and Gommorrah.

"Lord, if there are only 20 just men in the Cities won't you spare them destruction?"

"OK Abraham, if there are 20 . . ."

". . . . if there are 10"

"Yes, Abraham . . ."

And then Abraham hit God's least acceptable result. He (God) made sure those that had an ounce of possibility in them, out of town and then he went nuclear . . . and this wasn't all that long after he wiped out the entire earth with a flood.

The Bible says that God has a temper, but it also shows on numerous occasions that he can be successfully bargained with.

In the New Testament, The Apostle Paul took the Jewish Religion and the story of Jesus to the Greeks and Ephesians and a bunch of other people on his tours north and west of Israel. His entire purpose and message was persuasive.

Paul would compliment the heathens on their religiousness and devotion to their Gods, he'd build rapport and then come in with a message about the Unknown God and then record that he "successfully persuaded many that day."

Persuasion is what caused us to develop language in the first place. As a species we needed stuff. We learned to speak so we could ask for help in getting that stuff.

Persuasion is simply the stuff of life.

Subliminal persuasion is the experience you have when you aren't completely aware of everyone popping 20 dollar bills in the collection basket, you have a 10 but for some reason you decide to dig for another 10 and make it twenty.

A significant percentage of the actions you take are because something you were not consciously aware of caused you or primed (prepared you unconsciously) to act in a specific fashion.

"Subliminal" can mean "invisible" or "covert" but it can also mean . . . what it means . . . stimuli that you are not aware of.

In the last decade more research has been done on subliminal and supraliminal messages than the previous century before.

We now know that audio subliminal messaging is a great scam and that video messages designed to subliminally persuade because they simply don't work how the brain accepts information. But scientists and researchers in subliminal persuasion now know what does prime and persuade people at the unconscious level.

We can cause someone to drink X over Y or X over not drinking at all.

And those things can be done while looking at a computer screen and having an image of the word "drink" revealed at a duration too short for conscious awareness to pick it up, even if you're "looking for it."

The research in subliminal messages is nothing short of mind blowing in potential. The ability to change short term behavior can assist in changing long term behavior. The ramifications are beyond measure in society.

Propaganda is persuasion on a large scale.

I used to tell audiences, "I have propaganda at the back of the room. Please feel free to pick it up, check it out and. . . ."

One day a Jewish man came up to me and he was angry. Suggested that I was supporting evil.

Why?

Because I used the word, "propaganda."

I told him that while I could appreciate his point of view, there is nothing special about the word "propaganda." It's a message crafted to persuade more than one person. It's designed to persuade many about something I or the creator feels passionate about.

It certainly could refer to Hitlerian propaganda of the creation of the superior race but that is a pretty narrow minded view of a term that covers a lot of ground.

Commercials are propaganda. Marketing messages are propaganda. What your teacher teaches your kids and my kids teacher teaches my kids, is propaganda.

Propaganda is a necessary tool in a free society to differentiate yourself or your company or your religion or political ideology from another.

Propaganda is news with a spin and all news has a spin.

When I took journalism at the University of Wisconsin 25 years ago, I found the most difficult factor in writing news articles was being "objective." Today, of course, there is no such thing as objective news. Walter Cronkite is long gone from the news stage and the era of trying to get it "right" without a message attached to it is simply no longer possible due to how our world "runs."

If you want to watch your favorite TV shows and read your favorite newspaper, your favorite church publication, your favorite company newsletter, you will have to wade through "spin." They can't afford to publish without it. It's no longer possible to compete with objective news. Whether CNN, Fox or Al Jazeera, they all have an agenda. And that is the only way it can work in the 21st century.

Propaganda and subliminal persuasion in no way demands that Kevin Hogan gets something out of you being shaped by a message I send.

My intention here is to introduce to you Dave Lakhani.

Dave is a persuasion and propaganda expert. He's got a sharp mind and a quick eye for seeing through that which is muddy for the rest of us.

And Dave is a genius at crafting messages that are literally propaganda.

What I like about Dave is that part of his message is the same as mine. If you can reduce the necessity of being politically correct, you get closer to truth and reality. "Politically correct" is exactly what it says. It means that I refer to someone in a specific way so when people read things with other people in the room they know that everyone has been "protected" in the room from messages that show that people can think differently, freely, critically, with an opinion that might be different from an accepted group norm. i.e. "politically correct."

I've seen Dave intentionally raise eyebrows by saying things that even I wouldn't say on stage. That's in part because on those issues he's closer to the truth than I am and that he is willing to risk more for a response, his message and a lesson than I am.

That courage and intensity is something you will see woven with the genius and mission in this book.

This book will change your life, it will cause you to see things as you never have . . . but watch out. . . . Dave might have a hidden agenda that he isn't telling you about. . . .

—Kevin Hogan
Author of *The Psychology of Persuasion*
Minneapolis,
October 2007

PREFACE

Every day you take actions, buy products, and share beliefs and ideas without consciously thinking about them, and without going through a critical thinking path to come to a conclusion. You often do this without knowing where the belief or desire for the particular product or brand came from. In other words, you push the bar and the pellets come out; the retailer rings the bell and you salivate.

You've been subliminally persuaded . . . effectively, and completely.

This book was written for every entrepreneur, salesperson, advertiser, and small-business person who suspects there is a key to effectively moving markets and controlling consumers. I'm going to reveal the exact techniques you need to learn so you can have the greatest impact on the people you set out to persuade. I'm going to show you how to get a message across in an increasingly convoluted marketplace. I'm going to show you how to leverage the tools of mass influence to effectively influence the masses.

I've received a lot of questions about mass persuasion since I wrote my first book, *Persuasion: The Art of Getting What You Want.* This book is written to address those questions.

In this book, I define mass influence and subliminal persuasion (and I use the terms interchangeably in reference to persuading groups) as an attempt to purposefully and intentionally cause a group of people to take a predetermined action designed by the persuader, not the group themselves. This type of influence is most often seen in advertising, politics, propaganda, public relations, religion, literature, and movies. The goal is to get a defined audience to desire a product or have a belief that is consistent with the desired outcomes or goals of the persuader.

Getting you to take action is the goal of every marketer, politician, nonprofit, religious leader, and person with an agenda. I'm going to take you on a journey through the most efficient and effective techniques available to induce mass persuasion today.

You may find some of this material frightening.

You may ask, "Is this manipulation?" The answer is, of course —if that is your intent. How you use this material is entirely up to you. I hope you'll use it ethically and profitably.

When you look closely, you'll realize that in a market that is overstimulated and over-communicated you must do something different if you hope to succeed in gaining marketing compliance. You must leverage your ability to influence to achieve your goals. It isn't just good for you; it's also good for the economy and good for the world around us.

The point is that persuasion in all its forms is good.

Subliminal persuasion is right.

Subliminal persuasion works.

Subliminal persuasion clarifies, cuts through, and captures the essence of the consumer's pocketbook.

Persuasion, in all of its forms—persuading for life, for money, for love, for knowledge—has marked the upward surge of mankind.

And persuasion—mark my words—will not only save your job, and your income, but that other malfunctioning corporation called the World.

If you found yourself moved by the idea you just read, if you found that speech to be vaguely familiar, then you've experienced a low level of subliminal persuasion.

You may have correctly identified that the preceding dialog is a slightly changed version of the Gordon Gekko speech in the movie *Wall Street*. In the movie, Gordon Gekko said, "Greed . . . for the lack of a better word . . . is good" and that begins a speech that moves all of the shareholders of the fictional Teldar Paper Corporation. "Greed is good" may be the best known and most often quoted line from the movie.

But by slightly changing it, I'm able to build on the emotion, and the connection, even if you can't consciously make it and correctly identify it (confusion is a powerful subliminal persuasion technique). I'm able to trigger the feelings you had about how that speech made you feel the first time you heard it. In Neurolinguistic Programming (NLP) parlance, we call this firing an anchor, that is, providing a stimulus that initiates feelings previously connected to that stimulus.

Does it work? The answer, of course, is yes.

We tend to respond to the emotional content of our thoughts, feelings, and experiences. If we can tie that emotional content to actions we want others to take, then we have the potential for effective persuasion.

The chapters in this book walk you through exactly how to leverage the emotions, beliefs, and desires of the audiences you hope to persuade and lead them to consistently take the actions you want them to take.

Effectively.

Efficiently.

Ethically.

Profitably.

Persuasively.

I practice subliminal persuasion throughout the book to get you to take the actions I want you to take, so let me be clear about what I want you to do right up front. I want you to implement the ideas in this book profitably. I want you to live your life on your own terms. I want you to not have to give in to the demands of unreasonable people because you don't have another option. I want you to be able to get what you want by knowing exactly what it takes to get people who will take some action to take yours . . . because it is the best choice they can make.

My good friend, Glenn Dietzel, author of the book *Author and Grow Rich,* says that "writing is the doing part of thinking." Get out a pad of paper. My suggestion is that you go to a fine stationery store or to Barnes and Noble and buy a Moleskine notebook. It is the finest notebook you can buy. Use it for consolidating action steps and tactical execution plans. It was also the choice of Ernest Hemingway, Vincent van Gogh, Pablo Picasso, Bruce Chatwin, and your guide to all things persuasive, Dave Lakhani.

Keep your Moleskine next to you as you read this book. When you see something that you can use, write it down, not just a couple of words, but flesh it out. Write out exactly what audience you intend to influence and how you intend to apply the technique you've discovered.

Finally, take action. Implement the idea; don't let it lie flaccid in your notebook. Open the notebook and take the first step, watch your future spring to life.

I want you to remember what I tell everyone who attends my seminars:

"Implementation is everything—Money follows action!"

I look forward to seeing the action you take as you master the most profitable skill you'll learn in life.

Subliminal persuasion.

ACKNOWLEDGMENTS

While there are so many people who helped with this book and who have supported me through the process, none are more important than Matt Holt at John Wiley & Sons, Inc.

To Dr. Rachna Jain, Larry Beinhart, Ben Mack, Mickey Z., Joel Bauer, Martin Howey, Len Foley, Tellman Knudson, Eben Pagan, Joe Polish, and Mark Joyner: You guys are geniuses. Thanks for tolerating me and for all of your assistance with the book.

I'd like to especially thank Barbara Grassey for the editing work and the very funny comments. I just hope I got them all removed in the final edits. Barbara, thank you!

I'm especially thankful for my daughter, Austria, who told me that she was going to write a book when she is a big girl; nothing would make me more proud . . . unless she decides to do something totally different that makes her happy. Every time I look at this book, I'll remember all the times that she sat on my lap or next to me as I wrote and offered her own color commentary, the kind that can only come from a three-year-old. I aspire to be that persuasive and funny some day. Austi, when you read this later in life, know that Daddy loves you even more now as you read this than when I wrote it.

And, of course, I thank all of my family, my wife, Stephanie (who always knows the right time to go visit her sisters when I'm writing), my grandmother Edith Ramsey McManus, and my brothers, Bill Willard Jr. and Micah Willard. You guys have made my life an exceptional adventure; thank you.

Finally, to all my clients, past, present, and future. It is really the experiences I have with you that make these books possible.

1

CREATING
MESSAGE
CONTAGION

Ideas have to be wedded to action; if there is no sex, no vitality in them, there is no action.

— Henry Miller

This is a book that walks a very fine line. My publisher, with whom I have a tremendous relationship, wouldn't publish the book I wanted this to be because it was too edgy, too dangerous. So, I'm going to reveal the most cutting edge subliminal persuasion techniques, anyway; I'm going to expose what makes people make decisions; and I'm going to reveal how to control their thinking and behavior as it relates to buying your products and services. I'm going to draw the shortest line between where you are and the information you really want. If I do my job right, you'll find yourself exposed to some of the most profitable thinking in sales, marketing, advertising, and persuasion today. And, you'll be reading this because my publisher will agree that I took off enough of the edge without losing the value of the content.

Some ideas are too dangerous for polite company, but the last time I checked, your livelihood and mine was a deadly serious game, one we all hope to win.

You are about enter the arena of the winner, and you'll experience firsthand how those people who control the world around them think, how they act, and what tools of success they leverage to get what they want from you and from me.

THE ESSENCE OF SUBLIMINAL PERSUASION IS THE MESSAGE: THE MESSAGE YOUR AUDIENCE HEARS, RECEIVES, AND EXPERIENCES AS BEING TRUE

Persuasion is about messaging one-to-one or one-to-many. Subliminal persuasion occurs when you are able to successfully implant a message in the mind of a person or group of people whom you target for change without their conscious evaluation of the change, and encourage them to spread the idea organically to their associates.

Subliminal persuasion is about getting people to change their minds, to change their beliefs, and to accept new information as not only being correct, but having the necessity to spread.

Advertising, marketing, movie making, public relations, propaganda, negotiation, and religion all rely on subliminal persuasion.

The focus of this book is to teach you how to subliminally persuade the masses to take the actions you want them to take, to buy your products, services, and ideas. I'm going to teach you how to use this information ethically, but the decision will ultimately be up to you as to how you leverage this material. I'll hold nothing back.

Because ideas spread through exposure, you'll find yourself compelled to share what you learn, to leverage what you learn here. The more you expose yourself to these ideas, and the more you expose others to them, the more effective you become.

Subliminal persuasion is a learned skill set that when fully learned and integrated, disappears into the area of competent competence; you don't have to think about it to do it, you just do it. And the more time you spend focused on experiencing, testing, and leveraging these ideas in your business, your marketing, your advertising, and your sales processes, the more you'll spread the ideas that you must, so you can get more of whatever it is that you want . . . money, sex, power, fame, or anything else.

Getting messages and beliefs to spread is the primary goal of the persuader. The extent to which you can get people to accept your ideas preemptively will determine how effective your persuasive process will be. Also, the extent to which you can leverage, combine, or attach to existing beliefs, fears, anxieties, and facts will determine how overtly or covertly persuasive you need to be.

In mass influence, too much emphasis is often put on the individual at the beginning of the process. In fact, to be effective at subliminally persuading the group, you must first understand the underlying beliefs, motivations, and desires of the group as a whole. You must also carefully define which group you are going to persuade.

To be a highly effective subliminal persuader, you must know whom it is you intend to persuade. When governments use propaganda and other mass influence techniques to create changes in the beliefs of a populace, they first examine who will most easily accept the new information, whose paradigm the narrative best fits. They then create a powerful story and present it to the audience. They give them just enough evidence in the beginning that the people who *want* to believe the information will. Then, once they've bought in, everything else is a much easier sell and it sounds like something they've already heard, thereby subverting critical thinking.

HOW MESSAGES ARE SPREAD AND ACCEPTED

As human beings, we are programmed to spread messages; it is a condition of our humanity and our survival. We either consciously or subconsciously process the messages we receive, depending on the relevancy of the message we receive. The more closely the message matches our schema, the less conscious deconstruction is required. The more it motivates us in some way toward a better ideal, self, community, or universe, the more likely we are to spread it.

Ideas are spread when they are charged with emotion or meaning. They spread fastest when they are controversial, when they cast stones at our enemies, when they are motivational, when they promise salvation, or when they relieve a pressing pain that someone or a group is experiencing. In the wake of the September 11th tragedy, Americans were highly charged and looking for an enemy to strike back at. Regardless of your political view of the Iraq war, any enemy would do at that point; we simply needed to vent some anger on a deserving enemy. In that moment, there were many easy targets that could be painted as an enemy and a very strong cause-and-effect connection that could be made in the minds of most people by simply connecting the event with the enemy. The message spread and the persuasion occurred. But the idea that led to the connection and the persuasion occurred much earlier than September 11th.

As humans, the first way persuasive messages spread are from parent to child. The parents pass on beliefs and ideals that are presented as a set of truths. The child accepts the message and, in most cases, adopts the message as being the truth, models it, and makes it a piece of the construct by which the child will live his life and interpret the world around him. There are other relationships in life when beliefs are built and approximate the intensity of the child-parent message transmission. They are:

Educator-Student Relationship
Employer-Employee Relationship
Parish-Parishioner Relationship
Intimate-Significant Other Relationship

By studying and understanding the messages that were spread in these relationships as they relate to the change in belief you hope to create, you will better be able to create a message that will be accepted and passed along as a truism. Subliminal persuasion will have occurred.

Subliminal Sales Secret

To persuade subliminally, craft a message that matches the reality of the audience you intend to persuade by tying it to beliefs, ideas, and behaviors learned in the parent-child idea transmission, in the educator-pupil transmission or the societal dictator-participant transmission. Subliminal persuasion occurs most seamlessly and deeply when you affect core beliefs and ideas. Those messages are also most quickly spread when they demonstrate something that you've always believed is not true and when it supports and builds on those beliefs.

What is the message you want your audience to believe and spread? How can you relate it to core beliefs that your audience already holds as being true? What are the three beliefs that your audience holds as being true? The more emotional the content of the belief, the more likely your message is to be accepted and spread.

If you hope to create long-term subliminal persuasion, you begin by creating messages that result in beliefs that parents will hold as being true and pass on to their children. Once you've sufficiently affected the beliefs of a couple of generations of parents, persuasion is no longer necessary, because your message has moved from idea to what is now believed to be fact. Subliminal persuasion in business is a long-term proposition: What messages should the parents, educators, significant others, and religious leaders be learning and spreading to their children?

Urban myths are one of the best examples of messages being spread organically. The components of a good urban legend that will spread are the same as the components of an idea that will take off in a community of people whom you are influencing. Those components are:

1. A vivid and powerful story that plays on a preexisting belief or fear, or that creates the possibility of something that could be true.
2. The telling is done in a very vivid way that evokes urgency and plays on the beliefs or fears that already exist.
3. The story is typically reported by someone who presents the information as being true (whether it is or whether they know it is or not). Social proof is leveraged or implied.
4. The receiver has a similar reaction to the content of the story and because of the emotional impact of the story, maintains it at the top of the mind, and anchors the story in memory so that, in context, the anchor is fired and the story comes to mind. (More about anchoring later).
5. The receiver becomes the mouthpiece and spreads the story.

In subliminally persuading the masses, the process looks very similar.

1. Create a powerful hook, an idea that is intuitively accepted by the receiver. The hook may come in the form of a headline or sound bite that encapsulates the idea itself.
2. Set the presumption that the information is accurate by linking it to quantifiable evidence, trusted people, places, or things. Leverage social proof.
3. Tell the story with great gusto, make it vivid, emotionally appealing, and build big word pictures that people can dive in to.

4. Encourage interaction with the storyteller and encourage the next action. The more interactive he is with you and your message, the more persuaded he becomes.

Howard Gossage, the so-called Socrates of San Francisco and adman extraordinaire, created an ad for the Sierra Club to oppose "The Flooding of the Grand Canyon." His ad said "Now Only You Can Save the Grand Canyon from Being Flooded . . . for Profit." The copy goes on to talk about how a congressional bill would permit the building of two dams on the Colorado River and create a fluctuating shoreline based on hydroelectric needs, which would cause the Colorado River to become still water.

Gossage's ad was very effective. He encouraged people to get involved, and to spread the message by including seven coupons: one to join the Sierra Club, make a donation, or ask for more information; the rest were preaddressed to the president of the United States, the secretary of the interior, the member of Congress sponsoring the bill, the message recipient's representative in Congress, and two U.S. senators.

The ad was subliminally persuasive because it sold conservation through outrage. It was effective on two fronts. The bill didn't pass and the Sierra Club's membership jumped from 35,000 members to 50,000 members in six months. No one wants to see the Grand Canyon turned into a muddy lake (a future ad asked "Should We Also Flood the Sistine Chapel so Tourists Can Get Nearer the Ceiling?"). So, people wrote in and challenged the bill and they became conservationists in the meantime.

Subliminal persuasion is often effective because the message that is spread (in the case of Gossage, conservation) is not the obvious call to action. Cults never say, "Please join us; we are destructive." They offer something that is easily palatable and introduce you to a more controversial experience later (conservationism, like environmentalism today, was not an easy sell).

How can you make your message viral by leveraging the urban legend process, and how can you create a story in a story? Look carefully at your marketing, advertising, and public relations messages and see how you can carefully fold your core message inside something that is more easily palatable.

Volvo does an exceptional job of selling cars by wrapping their higher-priced cars in a story of safety. Whether you own a Volvo or not, you likely regularly use it as the standard of safety against which other cars are judged. Most people, when asked which brand of cars are the safest, will answer Volvo. Volvo never focuses on price, competition, or style (their cars are not that attractive); they focus on how important it is for a child to be safe in a crash, a message that is passed from parent to child as a fundamental truth about survivability. The message inside the message, though, is to buy a car that doesn't have high aesthetic desirability and costs more to do the same as the cool cars do, which is to get you from one place to another.

The process is really no different if you are subliminally persuasive in person. You craft a persuasive story that engages the emotions, tell it with passion, get people involved, and fold the most intense request inside an idea that is easy to understand. The folded idea is implicit or a natural extension of the story you tell.

My definition of persuasion is helping people come to their own natural conclusion, which happens to be the one you want them to have . . . this is the essence of subliminal persuasion.

CONNECTING MESSAGES FOR MAXIMUM PERSUASIVENESS

For messages to spread and subliminally persuade, there has to be a continuity of messaging so that people receive the message often enough to accept it.

There are three types of memory that we will concern ourselves with as they relate to subliminal persuasion.

Semantic Memory

The first type of memory is semantic memory. That is memory that is short-term in nature, echoic and that is diminished by sleep and short periods of time when the information is not repeated. This short-term memory must be impacted when you want people to take an instant action. The more charged the event around the memory, the more likely you are to remember it. If a beautiful woman gives you her phone number, you are much more likely to remember it than a list of things to pick up at the store. But if you don't write the woman's number down quickly, you'll lose it. When you are creating messages that you want to spread and building big ideas, you must go beyond this short-term memory and the only way to bypass it is through repetition. The more people are exposed to a message in a short period of time the more it moves from short-term memory into long-term procedural memory.

Episodic Memory

Episodic memory is grouped memories, memories of things, times, or places. For example, you remember Disneyland if you went, but don't have a moment-by-moment recall of what happened. You do have a grouping of memories that you relate and that create a certain set of experiences and emotions when you bring the episode in your life to mind. Semantic and episodic memories make up one of the two major divisions of memory called declarative memory. Declarative memory includes those memories that can be consciously discussed; they tend to be facts.

Procedural Memory

Procedural memory is the third type of memory and also the second general division of memory. Procedural memory is long-term memory, where processes, skills, and procedures are stored. Procedural memory is also referred to as implicit memory, and is often not easy to verbalize, but the process and procedures stored can be performed without consciously thinking about them. Strategies for making good buying decisions, motivational strategies, and so forth, are procedural memories.

Subliminal Sales Secret

If you want to get people to take an immediate action, you need to focus on affecting short-term semantic memory. Repetition combined with emotion, urgency, and scarcity will work to create an intense impact that will result in holding the idea in mind long enough to take the prescribed action.

When you want to condition an audience that may not have an immediate need for, or is resistant to, your product,

(continued)

(continued)

service, or idea, you need to connect memories, ideas, desires, actions, and beliefs to create new conclusions, which become emotional desires and beliefs. Once an idea becomes a belief, it moves to long-term procedural memory, where beliefs are held. When you can create an event or situation that connects the belief or procedural memory to create a new episodic memory, you reinforce the long-term memory, and encoding messages that are accepted subliminally is very easy. When you present information that fits the person or group you are persuading, you implant below the radar; acceptance and compliance are much more likely.

Another memory key that you can leverage is expectation. We all experience information through a set of filters that we have developed and have stored in our procedural memory and we view the world through these series of filters. We also attach the descriptions derived from our filters to situations, experiences, or people that tend to fit our expectations. So, for example, if I hold a belief that all skateboarders are not smart and cause problems, I'll see all skateboarders through that filter and find the support of my belief and that filter, not the exception. If I do find the exception, I'll identify it as an exception and probably view it as something that is going to change to fit my belief or schema.

I'm going to discuss beliefs, how they form, and how they propagate in another chapter. For now, leverage the idea that if you present information that is congruent with a belief, with a procedural memory, it is much more likely to be accepted without conscious scrutiny. Reducing the need for critical thinking and encouraging acceptance is one of your overriding goals as a subliminal persuader.

Message contagion happens when you focus on creating powerful messages that affect the group at a deeply subconscious level where their procedural memories lie.

Individuals and groups spread messages when they receive messages that are highly emotionally charged that are congruent with the deep-seated memories and beliefs of the intended audience.

For example, it is very tempting to make an analogy about the Iraq war right now because current polls show over 65 percent (as of this writing) of you reading this book are opposed to our involvement in the war. By leveraging those beliefs, I could either polarize you, and focus only on the ones who support the war, or I could send a message that polarizes those of you who don't. Either way, I'd become more acceptable to either audience by the message I send. If I create a message that you strongly agree with and makes an interesting argument, you are much more likely to store that message and share it with others.

But I'm not interested in debating the war, so let's look at something more practical and relevant to persuading the masses profitably.

ORGANICS

Let's look at what grocers and growers have done to create a new, very profitable subsegment of products in your grocery store.

Organics have been available for many years but were largely the food preferred by a very small segment of the population.

As food prices began to reach fairly fixed levels of profitability, marketers were tasked with creating more profitable categories. The marketers started by leveraging a belief (which may or may not be true) that the food we eat today contains fewer nutrients than foods produced 30 years ago.

The ideas were spread by creating stories in the media, in the grocery store ads, and in the customer loyalty newsletter that promoted the idea. The stories were made plausible by pointing out that the food you eat today, if you are a 30-year-old adult, does not taste the same as it did when you were a child. Episodic memory is fully leveraged, memories of your youth and Mom's home cooking come to mind and sure enough, the food doesn't taste the way it used to. Tomatoes grown the hydroponic way taste less robust than the ones you grow in your garden because they are grown in environments packed with chemicals. The stories provide research that seems likely but is rarely attributed to a reliable source, but you don't notice because the message-to-schema match is perfect. Food you eat today tastes different from the food of your childhood and those messages about how food should taste passed from parent to child are the most valuable, and they are shared values. Other people you talk to agree that the food you eat today tastes different. It makes for great water cooler conversation. So, the core idea is that food today is worse than food 30 years ago. You are hooked. Making the move from vegetables to milk and meat is a very simple process. Slightly altering the packaging to indicate something is *natural* or *organically* raised makes paying a little more a smart decision, because everyone knows that food 30 years ago must have been more organic. You buy the eggs with the Omega 3 added, and you get the milk that is organic, because you assume that it is from cows that from birth have never been exposed to chemicals that could harm you.

Without thinking, you spread the word that the organics you consume are better because . . . you got it, they taste better (read *different*).

The subliminal persuasion has occurred. You don't ask what the standards are to call something organic, you simply accept the idea that if it tastes different and the manufacturer calls it something that should be good for you, that it is. You've been persuaded and weren't even aware of it and you've become a willing evangelist, an unpaid marketer who endorses the idea that increases corporate profitability dramatically and raises your food bill.

But eventually, you may begin to question whether the decision you made was really right. Something might raise a little red flag. But that is okay, because here comes round two.

Once you buy in to the idea that organics are better for you, the next step is to hit you where you live. You drive a nice car, you provide your children with the very best possible life, you work a little harder, invest a little better, and do a little better than your neighbors. The competition goes right to the refrigerator and the pocketbook; the new status symbol of the millennium is the food you feed your family. The best families eat the best foods and the best foods are organics. Even if they come from a prepared meal created in a microwave oven.

The messaging is complete and the masses have complied. If you aren't eating organics, you know you should be and feel bad that you don't, so you eat them when you can.

The next step? Self-designed nutritional choices. My company, Bold Approach, is working with one of the nation's top specialty fertilizer producers and hydroponics manufacturer to create the ultimate status symbol, homegrown organics that produce year-round. As you begin to hear more and more about people growing their own salads and veggies year-round in their garage or extra closet, you'll know that our messaging is working, too.

It'll be complete when you have your own hydroponics setup in your garage and are feeding your family the way they deserve to eat, with food that is as hearty and wholesome as the food you and I used to readily be able to get our hands on at the local family-owned grocery store.

What you eat matters, where it comes from matters, and the ultimate expression of self-actualization is to choose the level of nutrients you'll consume today more cost-effectively and more satisfyingly by simply going to your own grocery store, the one in your garage.

When you set out to change the minds of the masses or the individual, start with a message that harnesses the power of stored memories and beliefs. Build on those beliefs and introduce them to the logical extension of their current representation of the world around them. Encourage them to share the information, talk to their friends about it, and become involved with the message itself.

Engagement equals action; action is the best indicator of subliminal compliance. Persuasion is assured.

Implementation Is Everything

Money Follows Action

If writing is the doing part of thinking, action is the creating part of profit. Each section of this book will have action steps for you to take so that you can ultimately build your own black

---

book of effective subliminal persuasion strategies and tactics that will ensure your success.

1. Clearly identify the outcome you want from your persuasive efforts. The more specific and clearer you are, the easier developing message contagion is.

2. Identify the episodic memories that the target audience is most likely to have, identify which beliefs currently exist as procedural memories that direct their actions and make up their filters of reality. This can best be accomplished through
   - Research
   - Direct Questioning
   - Personal Experience (If, in fact, you are truly representative of your target market. Most marketers are not, even when they fit the demographic.)
   - Observation
   - Focus Groups

3. Develop messages that are congruent with the memories and beliefs of your target audience and take them to the next logical level. Make the stories emotional and believable, and tell them what to look for (food tastes different from the way it did 30 years ago). Encourage them to get involved, tie in emotion or beliefs that were created at the earliest stages in their life or in the most emotionally impactful relationships discussed earlier.

4. Begin spreading your message one-to-one and one-to-many. Set up a figurehead, a spokesperson who can be the face of the message. Create a persona that is powerful and persuasive (See *Persuasion: The Art of Getting What You Want*
   (continued)

(continued)

for details on creating a persuasive persona). To ensure the deepest audience penetration and the most effective persuasion, create message contagion by injecting your message here:

- Mass Media—PR, Advertising, Applied Propaganda.
- Influence Groups—Direct Marketing, Public Speaking, Networking Groups, Business and Religious Organizations.
- One-on-One—Use the Urban Myth Model. Spread the message directly to key influencers (bloggers, writers, movie makers, politicians, corporate marketers, gossips, paparazzi).
- Nontraditional media—web sites, blogs created to support your message, viral videos on Google and YouTube.

5. Evaluate the response to your message and continue to create as many messages as necessary and put them into circulation as are required to make the message spread and accepted. Massage your messages to make them more attractive on the basis of their effectiveness and the feedback you get, and rerelease the new messages with the new spin for maximum effectiveness.

I'm going to give you in many chapters essential complementary study materials that you should acquire and consume immediately. Build a library of the most powerful subliminal persuasion ideas. Volume one will be this book, volume two will be your Moleskine full of your ideas, and the essential further study material that I share will make up the rest of the library.

ESSENTIAL FURTHER STUDY

Books

Think Two Products Ahead—Ben Mack (Wiley, 2007)
Fog Facts—Larry Beinhart (Nation Books, 2006)
Thought Contagion—Aaron Lynch (Basic Books, 1996)

Viral Video and Web Sites

The Bionic Burger: thebestdayever.com/burger.htm

Movies

Thank You For Smoking—Twentieth Century Fox, 2006

2

LEVERAGE APPLIED PROPAGANDA

The twentieth century has been characterized by three developments of great political importance: the growth of democracy, the growth of corporate power, and the growth of corporate propaganda as a means of protecting corporate power against democracy.

— Australian scholar Alex Carey

SUBLIMINAL SELLING SECRET

Creating your own vocabulary is a powerful subliminal persuasion tool. Creating new names or renaming the commonplace can make something appear very powerful and new. For example, I specifically chose to call public relations Applied Propaganda because that is what it really is.

Propaganda is a very highly charged word. Some people will assume that I'm talking about the intentional misleading of an audience. Others will assume I'm talking about mass education through the media. Both will take something away. But when I add the word *applied,* it causes you to pause and think, and it may even be a new construct that you can find yourself comfortable with.

Work hard to create precise word pictures that clearly identify who you are and what you do. Allow people to pick up your vocabulary and use it. Encourage your audience to be on the inside by using your specific language as a means of identifying one another.

But whatever you do, discuss how to use Applied Propaganda in your business.

Many people will find this chapter discomfiting and frightening because of the content. Stick with it, though. You'll see the effectiveness and ethical application of this chapter by the end. But to get you there, I need to take you through a history of propaganda so that you can learn my unique version of public relations, which I call *Applied Propaganda.*

If a given market has the capability to supply a neverending array of products, ideologies, concepts, and goods, how can we ultimately make our choices? What persuades enthusiastic and willing consumers like us to select Coke or Pepsi, McDonald's or Burger King, MasterCard or Visa, Crest or Colgate, Letterman or Leno?

Bigger picture: What makes us believe we actually *need* any of these commodities in the first place? The easy answer, of course, is *advertising.* We see the commercials, we hum the jingles, we even pay good money to adorn our bodies with clothing bearing corporate logos. Clearly, the many billions of dollars spent each year on advertising profoundly influence our lives. But there's also a parallel industry—albeit with a much lower profile.

"In societies like ours, corporate propaganda is delivered through advertising and public relations," says author and environmentalist Derrick Jensen. Advertising is a very overt attempt at persuading. The person or company who creates an advertisement is fully focused on creating an inducement that you will respond positively to. There is no exception based on what is being sold: ideas, services, or products. Applied Propaganda, on the other hand, is disguised as information, and called *public relations*. When asked, most people will say that they are not regularly influenced by the news and even hold it in low regard for its accuracy; yet we often don't realize we are being influenced by public relations.

If alarms began ringing in your head upon reading the term *propaganda*, you're certainly not alone. Given the unspeakable lessons learned from Joseph Goebbels and Nazi Germany, *propaganda* is officially a dirty word. But when Edward Bernays— nephew of Sigmund Freud, public relations pioneer, and America's most innovative social engineer—got his start in the early twentieth century, it was a word less charged but equally as potent. In fact, Bernays unabashedly named one of his books *Propaganda*.

"Edward Bernays was surely one of the most amazing and influential characters of the twentieth century," explains John Stauber, co-author of *Toxic Sludge is Good for You: Lies, Damn Lies, and Public Relations*. "He was a nephew of Sigmund Freud and helped to popularize Freudianism in the U.S. Later, he used his relation to Freud to promote himself. And from his uncle's psychoanalysis techniques, Bernays developed a scientific method of managing behavior, to which he gave the name 'public relations.'" The Vienna-born Bernays was heavily influenced, of course, by his uncle's work, but it was in the service of war that he helped shape what we call public relations today.

War has always been a proving ground for the development and dissemination of propaganda. Some of the most powerful lessons in managing the human perception of ideas comes from the selling of war. War sells the most costly idea of all, that there is something you should be willing to give your life for that is not you or your family. In what PR watchdog John Stauber calls "perhaps the most effective job of large-scale war propaganda which the world has ever witnessed," the Committee on Public Information, run by veteran newspaperman George Creel with the help of others like Edward Bernays, used all available forms of media to promote the noble purpose behind World War I: *To keep the world safe for democracy.* The average American was notoriously wary of any hint of their country entering the bloody conflict. "The country was becoming formally more democratic," notes linguist and social critic Noam Chomsky. "A lot more people were able to vote and that sort of thing. The country was becoming wealthier and more people could participate and a lot of new immigrants were coming in, and so on. So what do you do? It's going to be harder to run things as a private club. Therefore, obviously, you have to control what people think." As a result, men like Creel and Bernays were called upon to change some minds by leveraging one of the most powerful subliminal persuaders, public relations.

The Creel Committee (as it came to be known) was the first government agency for outright propaganda in U.S. history; it published 75 million books and pamphlets, had 250 paid employees, and mobilized 75,000 volunteer speakers known as "four-minute men," who delivered their pro-war messages in churches, theaters, and other places of civic gatherings. The idea, of course, was to give the war effort a positive spin. To do so, the nation had to be convinced that doing their part to support global military conflict on a scale never before seen was indeed a good idea. "It is not merely an army that we must train and shape for war," President Woodrow Wilson declared at the time, "it is an entire nation." The age of manipulated public opinion had begun in earnest.

Although Wilson won reelection in 1916 on a promise of peace, it wasn't long before he severed diplomatic relations with Germany and proposed arming U.S. merchant ships— even without congressional authority. Upon the congressional declaration of war on Germany in April 1917, the president proclaimed, "Conformity will be the only virtue and any man who refuses to conform will have to pay the penalty."

In time, the masses got the message as demonstrated by these (and other) results:

- Fourteen states passed laws forbidding the teaching of the German language
- Iowa and South Dakota outlawed the use of German in public or on the telephone
- German-language books were ceremonially burned from coast to coast
- The Philadelphia Symphony and the New York Metropolitan Opera Company excluded Beethoven, Wagner, and other German composers from their programs
- German shepherds were renamed Alsatians
- Sauerkraut became known as "liberty cabbage"

Buoyed by the indisputable success of the Creel Committee and armed with the powerful psychoanalytical techniques of his Uncle Sigmund, Bernays set about shaping the American consciousness in a major way. "The conscious and intelligent manipulation of the organized habits and opinions of the masses is an important element in democratic society," he wrote to open his influential book, *Propaganda*. "Those who manipulate this unseen mechanism of society constitute an invisible government which is the true ruling power of our country. We are governed, our minds are molded, our tastes formed, our ideas suggested, largely by men we have never heard of. This is a logical result of the way in which our democratic society is organized. Vast numbers of human beings must cooperate in this manner if they are to live together as a smoothly functioning society."

Bernays's vision of a smoothly functioning society had a dominant economic component. As described by Tim Adams of the *London Observer*, Bernays "thought that the safest way of maintaining democracy was to distract people from dangerous political thought by letting them think that their real choices were as consumers." This focus on maintaining democracy led to the development of the consumer-driven marketplace of today. It also began the process of mental conditioning that as a subliminal persuader you must leverage. In our society today, most people define themselves by the things that they own, the cars that they drive, and the schools their children go to. Marketers who understand this deep conditioning are much more able to create messaging that will allow them to affect their audiences quickly, easily, and completely.

Subliminal Selling Secret

Research your target audience; understand how they see themselves. Leverage their beliefs about who they are in your messaging. If who they see themselves as is not powerful enough or does not allow for you to profitably build on the image, create a new one.

As Bernays created the perception of choice as a consumer, how can you create a perception of who your audience is? This, of course, requires a great deal of thinking, questioning, and research, but it is incredibly powerful.

A fine illustration of Bernays's approach involves his efforts—for the American Tobacco Company—to persuade women to take up cigarette smoking. His slogan, "Reach for a Lucky Instead of a Sweet," exploited women's fear about gaining weight (arguably a fear manufactured through previous advertising and public relations work). While Lucky Strike sales increased by 300 percent in the first year of Bernays's campaign, there was still one more barrier he needed to break down: smoking remained mostly taboo for "respectable" women.

This is where some watered-down Freud came in handy. As Bernays's biographer, Larry Tye, said, Bernays wanted to take his uncle's works and "popularize them into little ditties that housewives and others could relate to." With input from psychoanalyst A. A. Brill, Bernays conjured up the now-legendary scheme to reframe cigarettes as a symbol of freedom.

"During the 1929 Easter Parade," explains *New York Times* reporter Ron Chernow, "he had a troupe of fashionable ladies flounce down Fifth Avenue, conspicuously puffing their 'Torches

---

of Freedom,' as he had called cigarettes." As Chernow reports, Bernays augmented this successful stunt by lining up "neutral experts" to "applaud the benefits of smoking, all the while concealing the tobacco company's sponsorship of his activity."

Bernays was also concealing his knowledge of tobacco's deleterious effects. "As he hypocritically seduced American women into smoking, he was trying to wean his own wife from the nasty habit," Chernow continues. "His daughter, Anne Bernays, the novelist, recalls that whenever he discovered a pack of his wife's Parliaments, 'he'd pull them all out and just snap them like bones, just snap them in half and throw them in the toilet. He hated her smoking.'"

This applied propaganda tactic of reframing or spinning an issue is still widely used today but often for more altruistic ends. For example, when AIDS first reared its ugly head, it was quickly—and inaccurately—labeled a "gay disease." This categorization was not only erroneous but it also carried with it a dangerously negative stigma. To be diagnosed as HIV-positive was to risk one's reputation and livelihood at the very least. Efforts began to reframe the AIDS crisis—and it went much further than lighting a cigarette during the Easter Parade.

By publicizing the scope and range of the disease, AIDS inevitably came to be viewed (correctly) as a global health emergency that could be contained by education, not finger pointing and labeling. On the American Red Cross web site, this issue is addressed as such:

Question: Isn't AIDS a gay disease?
Answer: No. AIDS (a result of HIV infection) is caused by
   HIV, a virus that can infect people regardless of sexual

orientation. HIV can infect anyone who has sexual or blood-to-blood contact with an HIV-positive person. The virus can infect men, women, and children. Men who have sex with men or women and women who have sex with men or women are at risk if their partners have HIV infection. Correct and consistent use of latex (or poly-urethane if allergic to latex) condoms, however, greatly reduces the risk of transmission. Risk relates to what people do, not who they are.

"The global HIV/AIDS epidemic is an unprecedented crisis that requires an unprecedented response," adds former United Nations Secretary General Kofi Annan. "In particular, it requires solidarity—between the healthy and the sick, between rich and poor, and above all, between richer and poorer nations. We have 30 million orphans already. How many more do we have to get, to wake up?"

Appropriately, in a classic bit of Bernaysian persuasion, a simple, small red ribbon has come to represent the international effort of AIDS awareness, prevention, and education. While the deadly disease remains a clear and present danger, the applied propaganda movement to reframe how it is perceived has undoubtedly saved many lives.

Another common Bernays tactic was independent third-party endorsement. Asked by Beechnut Packing to increase their sales of bacon, Bernays conducted a survey of medical professionals ("America's leading physicians," he claimed). "He didn't just give them a wide open choice," says Larry Tye. "He defined the choice as: the rushed breakfast that people are eating today or the good, hardy, bacon and eggs breakfast?"

Framed in such a manner, the vast majority of doctors agreed that a good, hardy breakfast was superior to a rushed breakfast. Defining "hardy" as meaning bacon and eggs, Bernays publicized his survey results with great fanfare. His deceptive, yet innovative, strategy did much more than increase Beechnut's size of the bacon market; it expanded the market itself. "Modern propaganda," wrote Bernays, "is a consistent, enduring effort to create or shape events to influence the relations of the public to an enterprise, idea, or group." Thanks to this particular "enduring effort," bacon and eggs eventually developed into the All-American breakfast.

In the twenty-first century, the concept of an independent third-party endorsement can have a much healthier connotation. For example, those seeking foods that are certified organic are apt to look for a third-party certification on the label. If you prefer your coffee to be "Fair Trade" certified, what better way to be sure than to ask that this is verified by a third party? Ironically, those opting for a "hardy," animal-free breakfast will often demand a certified vegan label on their food products.

An additional Bernays breakthrough involved creating what he termed *ballyhoo* and he brought it all the way from Broadway to the White House. Calvin Coolidge became the thirtieth president when Warren G. Harding died in 1923. Coolidge was elected in his own right 15 months later. While an effective public speaker, Coolidge was economical with his words in private and soon earned the nickname "Silent Cal."

His legendary reticence allegedly garnered the curiosity of the popular writer and socialite Dorothy Parker. As the story goes, Parker was seated next to the uncommunicative president at a dinner party. She turned to him and loudly declared,

"Mr. Coolidge, I've made a bet against a fellow who said it was impossible to get more than two words out of you." He famously replied: "You lose." (Upon being told of Coolidge's death in 1933, Parker famously replied, "How can they tell?")

"The words of a president have an enormous weight," Coolidge said, "and ought not to be used indiscriminately." Renowned newspaperman Walter Lippmann saw genius in Coolidge's laid-back, taciturn style. "This active inactivity suits the mood and certain of the needs of the country admirably," said Lippmann. "It suits all the business interests which want to be let alone. . . . And it suits all those who have become convinced that government in this country has become dangerously complicated and top-heavy."

Edward Bernays saw things a little differently from Lippmann. To him, Silent Cal was "practically inarticulate, and no movement of any kind agitated his deadpan face." Thus, when asked to help enhance and liven up the president's image and demonstrate his "warm, sympathetic personality," Bernays hit upon the concept of a "photo op." He invited vaudeville stars to the White House because "stage people symbolize warmth, extroversion, and Bohemian camaraderie."

A group that included Al Jolson, Ed Wynn, the Dolly Sisters, Charlotte Greenwood, and Raymond Hitchcock arrived for a pancake breakfast—and you can be certain there were plenty of cameras present. "I have met you all across the footlights," welcomed Mrs. Coolidge, "but it's not the same as greeting you here."

The star power worked (was there ever any doubt?) and the next day's newspaper headlines included: "Actor Eats Cake with the Coolidges," "President Nearly Laughs," and

"Guests Crack Dignified Jokes, Sing Songs, and Pledge to Support Coolidge."

"Al Gore is, uh, not a dynamic speaker," says late night comedian, David Letterman. "Halfway through his speech, squirrels were climbing on him." So it went for the former vice president for the vast majority of his political career. Since losing the 2000 presidential election, however, Gore has reshaped his image with a little ballyhoo of own and, in the process, taught the world about global warming.

Thanks to star power that would have Mrs. Coolidge's head spinning, Al Gore has gone from bore to prophet. By enlisting celebrities and other high profile groups to help him spread the word about climate change, he has ended up with an Oscar-winning documentary, *An Inconvenient Truth;* the Nobel Peace Prize; and a series of consciousness-raising concerts called "Live Earth." On July 7, 2007, millions of people around the world participated in what was essentially a global wake-up call, orchestrated by a man once perceived to be a bore.

Today, publicity stunts like the Live Earth concerts are more commonly known as *media events* or *photo ops,* but Bernays liked to call them *overt acts.* As demonstrated by the events leading up to the 1954 U.S.-sponsored coup in Guatemala, Edward Bernays had nothing against *covert* acts, either.

"He believed, and argued to Eisenhower, that fear of communists should be induced and encouraged, because by unleashing irrational fears, it would make Americans loyal to the state and to capitalism," writes Tim Adams, in the *London Observer.*

The United Fruit Historical Society web site offers an instructive chronology of the United Fruit Company (now Chiquita). The entries include:

1901: The government of Guatemala hires United Fruit Company to manage the country's national postal service.

1904: Guatemalan dictator Manuel Estrada Cabrera grants United Fruit a 99-year concession to construct and maintain the country's main rail line from Guatemala City to Puerto Barrios.

1924: The Guatemalan government gives a concession to the United Fruit Company for all the uncultivated lands in a 100-square-kilometer territory.

United Fruit's domination of this Central American nation was challenged when, in a landslide victory, Jacobo Arbenz was freely and fairly elected president of Guatemala in 1951. Wishing to transform his country "from a backward country with a predominantly feudal economy to a modern capitalist state," Arbenz's modest reforms and his legalizing of the Communist Party were frowned upon in U.S. business circles. The Arbenz government became the target of a U.S. public relations campaign headed by none other than Edward Bernays. "As I anticipated," the PR pioneer boasted, "public interest in the Caribbean skyrocketed in this country."

Two years after Arbenz became president, *Life* magazine featured a piece on his "Red" land reforms, claiming that a nation just "two hours bombing time from the Panama Canal" was "openly and diligently toiling to create a Communist state." It mattered little that the U.S.S.R didn't even maintain diplomatic relations with Guatemala; the Cold War was in effect. Ever on the lookout for that invaluable pretext, the U.S. business class scored a public relations coup when Arbenz expropriated some unused land controlled by the United Fruit Company. His payment offer was predictably deemed inappropriate.

"If they gave a gold piece for every banana," Secretary of State John Foster Dulles clarified, "the problem would still be Communist infiltration."

"Articles began appearing in the *New York Times,* the *New York Herald Tribune,* the *Atlantic Monthly, Time, Newsweek,* the *New Leader,* and other publications, all discussing the growing influence of Guatemala's Communists," writes Larry Tye, Bernays's biographer. "The fact that liberal journals like *The Nation* were also coming around was especially satisfying to Bernays, who believed that winning the liberals over was essential. . . . At the same time, plans were under way to mail to American Legion posts and auxiliaries 300,000 copies of a brochure titled 'Communism in Guatemala—22 Facts.' "

Bernays's clandestine efforts led directly to a brutal military coup when the CIA put Operation Success into action. "A legally elected government was overthrown by an invasion force of mercenaries trained by the CIA at military bases in Honduras and Nicaragua and supported by four American fighter planes flown by American pilots," explains historian Howard Zinn.

Once in power, Colonel Carlos Castillo Armas, a man who was trained at Fort Leavenworth, Kansas, gave back the land to United Fruit, abolished the tax on interest and dividends to foreign investors, eliminated the secret ballot, and jailed thousands of political critics. The CIA coup ushered in 40 years of repression, resulting in more than 200,000 deaths and one of the most inhumane chapters of the twentieth century.

One of the most inhumane chapters of the still-young twenty-first century is the Darfur conflict. This complex crisis in the Darfur region of western Sudan is the result of decades of drought, desertification, overpopulation, and a raging civil war. The United Nations (UN) estimates that the conflict has left as many as 450,000 people dead, and as many as 2.5 million people displaced.

Advocacy groups such as Amnesty International have long attempted to focus world attention on this situation, but it wasn't until outgoing United Nations President and Humanitarian Coordinator for Sudan, Mukesh Kapila, called Darfur the "world's greatest humanitarian crisis" in 2004 that a movement emerged. In short order, Darfur was featured on MTV and shows like *The West Wing*. Celebrities like Green Day, Matt Damon, and George Clooney have worked to help bring attention to the conflict. Unlike the efforts to undermine democracy in Guatemala, the tools and techniques of persuasion are being exploited to mobilize people everywhere they live in the world.

HOW TO ETHICALLY AND EFFECTIVELY LEVERAGE APPLIED PROPAGANDA (WITHOUT ACTUALLY OVERTHROWING A DEMOCRATICALLY-ELECTED GOVERNMENT)

To have great poets, there must be great audiences, too.
— Walt Whitman

As you can see, in one form or another, Bernays's tactics of persuasion—for better and for worse—remain deeply rooted in contemporary American culture. This is true in politics and, of course, business. And that should include *your* business.

In the modern marketplace, almost all buyers and sellers have access to the same technology. Differentiating oneself in the midst of all the information changing hands at warp speed requires cleverness, creativity, and confidence (three characteristics Bernays had in spades). While many of us would be loathe to use the word *propaganda* to depict what we do to attract our audience, in a Bernaysian sense, it's an accurate description. When it comes down to it, one person's *propaganda* is another's *education* (and vice versa).

"Each of these nouns carries with it social and moral implications," wrote Bernays. "The only difference between *propaganda* and *education*, really, is in the point of view. The advocacy of what we believe in is education. The advocacy of what we don't believe in is propaganda."

What Bernays can teach today's marketer is indeed about *education*. In a market that is increasingly overstimulated and skeptical, you must use proven techniques to gain mass acceptance . . . and make the idea seem like it's that market audience's own. Reaching your target market in this manner takes audacity, but it's all for naught unless there is a story or lesson there to persuade that audience to consider your product or service. If you believe that what you have to offer has intrinsic value—*if it's about more than just profit*—you can ethically utilize propaganda to connect with a wider audience and to educate and inspire that audience once you have their attention.

Five Lessons We Can Learn from Edward Bernays

1. Recognize or create new markets

    Let's revisit the "hardy breakfast" positioning. Bernays did not content himself with getting his client, Beechnut, a larger share of the established bacon-buying population. Rather, his vision was bolder and ultimately, far more lucrative. He set out to drastically increase the actual number of Americans shopping for bacon and thus fashioned an entirely new market. Getting a bigger slice of the pie is fine, but Bernays took it to the next level: He created a larger pie.

Ask yourself: How many potential consumers are out there beyond perceived target markets and why aren't they being reached? What notions about our market can we create and leverage; what education can we provide that we currently are not?

By carefully looking at where your audience is today as determined by beliefs and experiences, you can often create a new experience that leads the market in a new way and leaves it forever changed. You not only create a new market identity but you create a niche in the marketplace that you fill before anyone else and become very difficult to knock out.

2. See with "new eyes"

If we were able to temporarily put aside the deceptive and unethical nature of Bernays's campaign to market cigarettes to women, we'd recognize a valuable lesson (besides *Don't smoke*). If Bernays had simply tried to address only the social taboo surrounding women and smoking, he would've had to go up against a deeply embedded societal belief (an immovable object if there ever was one). By looking at the issue from a fresh perspective, Bernays persuaded the average American to consider a new angle: women's liberation. The cigarettes became secondary to the "real" issue: equality. As author Marcel Proust once said, "The only real voyage of discovery consists not in seeking new landscapes but in having new eyes."

Ask yourself: What is sitting—undiscovered—right in front of me?

3. Act locally, think globally

Edward Bernays once wrote: "Ideas are sifted and opinions stereotyped in the neighborhood bridge club. Leaders assert their authority through community drives and amateur theatricals. Thousands of women may unconsciously belong to a sorority which follows the fashions set by a single society leader." Put into a more modern context: Individuals tend to follow trends. Marketers can exploit this straightforward reality in two primary ways:

a.) Help create a new trend

b.) Recognize an existing or emergent trend

Ask yourself: What development is lurking on the horizon that may affect my market, or what current trend has the potential to drive customers my way?

4. Get inside their heads

Being Sigmund Freud's nephew gave Bernays access to the cutting edge in psychoanalytical thought and methods of persuasion. Bernays's dissemination of Freud's ideas taught businesses, marketers, advertisers, entrepreneurs, and yes, government officials, that persuasion is rarely about offering what people need. A deeper understanding of humans—their hopes, fears, desires, and so forth—made it possible to offer them what they dream about and truly want.

Ask yourself: How does my product or service appeal to consumers on a deeper level, and how can I create emotional content to bring this appeal to the forefront?

5. Be relentless

"Modern propaganda," wrote Edward Bernays, "is a consistent, enduring effort to create or shape events to influence the relations of the public to an enterprise, idea or group." Repetition works. Patience works. "The truth has to be repeated," Pakistani scholar Eqbal Ahmed reminds us. "It doesn't become stale just because it has been told once. So keep repeating it. Don't bother about who has listened, who has not listened. . . . [T]he media and the other institutions of power are so powerful that telling the truth once is not enough. You've got to keep repeating different facts, prove the same point."

Ask yourself: Do I give up too easily or expect results too quickly?

THE APPLIED PROPAGANDA STRATEGY

In my first book, *Persuasion: The Art of Getting What You Want* (Wiley, 2005), I shared with you that the difference between persuasion and manipulation comes down to one word . . . *intent.* When using Applied Propaganda, intent remains a key component in deciding whether the message you are spreading is appropriate or not. It isn't my intention to ascertain for you whether it is or not, but I will ask that before you employ this highly effective strategy that you consider the following.

1. *Identify the people most susceptible to your message*—
   Subliminal persuasion, applied propaganda, and public relations work best when you initially target your
   audience carefully. The audience should be made up of
   people who are intensely curious about your offering.
   They may also be disenfranchised or feel left out. Your
   message should connect your audience to its other members and encourage connectors (those people who tend
   to reach out to others) to bridge the gap with the disenfranchised among your audience. Hermits are rarely the
   best to target with this style of messaging.

2. *Break your message down to the most easily understood
   piece*—The key to inducing message contagion is to create
   small, easy to consume, and easy-to-pass-on messages that
   have high emotional impact. The more people feel (literally)
   that the message was directed at them and their beliefs, the
   more likely they are to internalize it and pass it on.

3. *Choose your media*—People will often tell me that if
   they get on Oprah, it would change their life because so
   many people would hear about what they are doing. The
   challenge, of course, is that if what they are doing is not
   of interest to Oprah's audience at large, you are in front
   of a lot of uninterested people. For example, if you work
   in a niche, it is often much better and more profitable to
   be in smaller, targeted media than to appeal to a larger
   crowd. Also, first choose media that are supportive of
   your ideas to develop a following before you take on
   the ones where contention may exist. Contention can
   be a powerful tool because conflict is a key component
   of every good and enduring story. But you need to be

prepared with an army of supporters and social proof before you take on a critic.

4. *Repeat your message as often as possible*—Beliefs develop as ideas become prevalent. The more people hear your messages in different places, the quicker acceptance occurs.

5. *Employ social proof*—Demonstrate the movement by showing others who are already doing it. When people see others doing something specific, particularly in the media and especially when it is interesting, they are more likely to repeat it. Use testimonials, examples, figureheads, and so on to provide social proof.

6. *Fully understand the public relations process*—By understanding exactly how to influence the media, you are better able to persuade your audience. Present the media with the information they need to spread your message in the format they want to receive it. Leverage new media (which I discuss in another chapter) to fully affect even the smallest niche audience.

7. *Create common knowledge by publicizing your media through advertising*—Let your audience know what is true by reminding them through advertising and spreading the message further.

You must have an ongoing effort to most effectively leverage the applied propaganda strategy. Public relations and applied propaganda work because they are constant. The message is received through multiple media time and time again, until it becomes common knowledge, a truism. The ability for the message receiver to accept the message, repeat it, and then act on it is the yardstick by which you'll measure successful implementation.

Subliminal Selling Secret *" SOUND BITES "*

Sound bites are a staple of public relations, and they should be a staple of every person who persuades. A sound bite is a concise, easy-to-understand statement that can be made quickly and with great impact. Sound bites tend to be around one or two sentences long.

The challenge that many people have with sound bites is that they feel that they can't communicate a complex idea in one or two simple sentences. But, communicating a complex idea in a sentence or two is not the purpose of a sound bite at all. The purpose is to gain attention, generate intense interest, or stop an idea in its tracks, nothing more.

The best sound bites are created by taking the most interesting, volatile, agreeable, or obvious piece of the idea or argument and showcasing it. The focus of the effort is to get people to instantly understand and accept what you are saying. Sound bites can also be used to unravel other people's logic and arguments in the media when they don't have time (and are often not prepared) to respond to well-thought-out brief statements that are complete. A famous and very useful sound bite came during a Reagan-Mondale presidential campaign debate in 1984. When Reagan's age was brought into question, he responded, "I will not make age an issue of this campaign. I'm not going to exploit, for political purposes, my opponent's youth and inexperience." Another famous sound bite came from Johnny Cochran, a defense attorney for O. J. Simpson in Simpson's widely publicized murder trial in reference to a

---

glove found at the crime scene. Cochran's famous sound bite was: "If it doesn't fit, you must acquit."

When used effectively in the media or even one-on-one, sound bites are subliminally persuasive because they are an idea that the mind can grasp and that are easily remembered. When people are overwhelmed and overcommunicated, they will much more easily grasp ideas that are to the point and easy to understand. Finally, sound bites work because they seem to not need any interpretation; they make sense and drive people toward what appears to be a logical conclusion.

If you are going to persuade or educate using Applied Propaganda, spend time creating your sound bites. It will be one of the most profitable things that you can do.

Here is an easy way to remember how to use applied propaganda. "When you educate, relate, and sedate, the masses feel great." Feel free to quote me on that.

Implementation Is Everything
Money Follows Action

Before you read the next chapter, take the following actions:

Use Bernay's tactic of "seeing with new eyes" and look for opportunities to spin your current argument in a new way. See how you can recast or pitch your product or service in an unexpected way. Tie in a social cause; appeal to people's sensitivities or sensibilities.

Develop a back-of-napkin strategy leveraging Applied Propaganda through the new media, blogs, online video, social

(continued)

(continued)

networking, wikis, and podcasts. The use of this free and oft-searched media is highly underused by most businesses today.

Begin thinking of your advertising and public relations efforts as education and see how it changes your efforts and propositions.

ESSENTIAL FURTHER STUDY

Books

Propaganda—Edward Bernays and Mark Crispin Miller (Ig Publishing, 2004)

Coercion—Douglas Rushkoff (Riverhead Books, 2000)

The Culture Code—Clotaire Rapaille (Broadway, 2006)

Viral Video and Web Sites

"The Century of the Self"—Adam Curtis: search video .google.com

Movies

Frontline: *The Persuaders* (PBS, 2004)

3

POSITION
AND PACKAGE
YOUR LEGEND

When the legend becomes fact, print the legend.
—from the movie *The Man Who Shot*
Liberty Valance, 1962

Positioning and packaging is creating a legendary message that meets the expectation of your target audience and gains persuasive compliance. I covered storytelling as a personal persuasion tool in my first book, but this chapter goes much deeper into the process. This is probably the most time-consuming subliminal persuasion tactic, but it is without question the one I'd never be without. This is the tactic that I start all consulting with.

People often ask me to explain the difference between positioning and packaging relative to packaging a company or an individual and the answer is, there really is none. The same reasons that positioning and packaging make subliminal persuasion more effective make you more effective both one-on-one as well as one on many.

In positioning and packaging a person, a company, or an idea, we are leveraging several critical factors:

1. *We are leveraging storytelling*—Stories are our oldest form of communication and the best stories are the ones that will transcend time.

2. *We are focusing on creating complementary models*—We are positioning and packaging ourselves, our ideas, and our businesses so they fit the schema of the person experiencing them. We are also positioning and packaging so that the story fits the timeless models of stories that people understand so that they understand how to consume and interpret them. We want to make the conclusion impossible to miss.

3. *We are creating a persona that is easily identifiable with you, your company, and your product or your service*—If you look at how politics has evolved, Republicans have taken on the persona of being conservative and Democrats liberal. For a politician to be effective in either party, he or she must have a persona that is congruent with the bigger identities of the party.

The goal is to deeply implant and leverage ideas in the subconscious where most thinking is done. Once we've made our impact on the subconscious appropriately, it is very easy to control the outcome of the messages we are sending.

Gerald Zaltman, author of *How Customers Think* (Harvard Business School Press, 2003), reporting on the work of Harvard professor and psychologist Jerome Kagan says that 95 percent of thinking occurs in our unconscious minds.

It is that thought stew from which we pull the ingredients to create our opinions and interpretations of events around us. Effective narratives enter that thought process effectively, mostly without conscious consideration and reside there waiting for us to pull them back up and leverage the information so we can make a decision. The subliminal persuader understands that the person making the decision mostly does not have an encyclopedic reference system for determining whether the information or ideas she receives are real or fictional. Therefore, when you create narratives, the more congruent they are, the more easily they are accepted as factual. This idea is so important (in reference to recovered memories) that in 1993, the American Psychiatric Association stated, "It is not known how to distinguish with complete accuracy memories based on true events from those derived from other sources."

When I was an undercover narcotics officer, one of my jobs was to help people create covers and backstories to back up their assumed identities. I was also responsible for helping them develop and encode the stories that they would tell in high-stress situations. We started with a very simple premise: The best lie is 90 percent true. You build the story using one's own first name. That was something they wouldn't have to worry about, and if someone shouted his name and he looked without thinking, it wouldn't be considered a tell, a clue that something was amiss. Start with your own true story when crafting your brand or persona.

In business, we are not creating fictional stories. The most effective marketers and persuaders are carefully crafting, positioning, and packaging stories and ideas to make them most believable and most credible to the public. The extent to which the positioning and packaging is effective will determine the ease with which the idea is accepted. Another word for this kind of messaging is *branding*. Your brand communicates with your customer at a very subliminal level and if the story your brand tells is a good one it becomes real in the mind of the consumer.

The idea of narrative and story as it relates to subliminal persuasion is just coming to the forefront, although it has existed unexplored for quite some time. Professional persuaders are just beginning to understand how to add storytelling to their arsenal.

Subliminal Selling Secret

I spoke with Larry Beinhart, the legendary author who wrote *Wag The Dog* and *Fog Facts,* both must-read books. I asked him for his take on narrative as a persuasive tool and he said, "Everything we think and do is the result of a narrative. We tell ourselves a story in our head about going to the store, getting milk and eggs, then going for some gas and grabbing our mail on the way in the door."

When you control the narrative, you control the outcome. Stories have the ending that the writer writes, not the ending that you necessarily want. It is up to you as a persuader to begin analyzing the stories you are telling so you can control the narrative in the mind of the person you are persuading.

Narratives also have higher recall than litanies. Stories are easier to remember because they are grouped and connected

---

ideas. One of the best memory strategies involves linking items together to create a narrative (often a very odd one) that allows you to flow from one item to the next in a long list.

Use stories and narrative when you write e-mails, when you talk to someone face to face, and when you are giving her a list of features and benefits. Rather than give a list, tell a story. The bonus is that she'll remember you better as well because she'll have connected with you on a more personal level.

DECONSTRUCTING YOUR CURRENT LEGEND

You must first understand the story you are telling so you can create a powerful narrative that will allow you to position and package yourself in the most efficient way.

Marketers will often say that their story is about things like price or selection or convenience. And they may, in fact, be right. But those are typically not the best stories to tell. More on that in a moment.

I want you to deconstruct your story by asking the following questions and writing down your answers. You'll need them as we move forward. This is where your Moleskine will come in handy; I use the mid-sized one with the elastic band and folder in the back.

1. What is the premise or the overarching moral statement of the story you are trying to tell?
2. Who, or what, is the focal point in your story?
3. What are the overriding emotions, memories, and beliefs that you are tying into the telling of the story?

4. What emotion are you trying to evoke with the story? What emotion *are* you evoking with the story?

5. What vital ideas are you communicating in your story?

6. What actions are the reader, listener, or viewer supposed to take?

Don't be surprised if you don't have good answers to all the questions; most people don't. But you will shortly. Narrative thinking and creation works amazingly well when you do have the answers, so let's take a look at how legends form for the purpose of building a legend that deeply influences the masses and allows them to readily identify you and with you.

CREATING YOUR LEGEND

When I consult with companies and individuals to create rapid consumer acceptance of the ideas they want to proliferate, I start by talking to them about the legend that they want to create.

Nearly always, the answer is, "We don't have a legend."

But that is never true. Your legend is based around what it is that you do better than anyone else, your specific skills, interpretations, applications, or abilities. It revolves around how you got into the position you are in now. But to get to the legend you must start in the beginning.

1. How did I get here?—You start building your legend by asking about how you got here. What unique path brought you here? No detail is too small, and more is better in the building of a legend; you can always pare back later.

In my case, I talk about growing up in a cult as my impetus to begin studying persuasion. I talk about the things that happened to me there. I build up the experience so that it is vivid and memorable. I connect it to experiences and beliefs people already have. My legend is persuasion; that is the one thing I always want associated with me.

2. What did I learn that others don't know?—Legends often do heroic things or they know things that no one else knows.

   Part of my legend is that I learned how to persuade and manipulate from my upbringing in a cult. I learned even more through a course of rigorous study that has lasted more than 25 years and continues to this day.

3. What do I stand for?—Legends have to stand for something. They have to be bigger than life because of what they do and the service they provide.

   My legend stands for truth and skills. Persuasion, not unethical manipulation, replicable skills that you can employ at will to get the things you want.

Once you have the basis for the legend there is one more component: building the narrative so that the legend can be transferred from person to person or from one to many.

ELEMENTS OF A SUBLIMINALLY PERSUASIVE STORY

The process I'm about to teach you is as old as stories themselves. If you study literature, mythology, the Bible, or some other religious text of your choice, you'll find stories follow a very similar structure.

Joseph Campbell, one of the world's greatest experts on mythology, termed these kinds of stories *The Hero's Journey*. Some of the best stories ever told, the Jesus story, *Star Wars*,

The DaVinci Code, all follow the Hero's Journey as the model for the construction of their stories.

I've altered the model slightly to fit the needs of the professional persuader.

THE MYTH MODEL

The meta-message of your story, or the ideological statement, is the conclusion you want someone to draw from the story. In the example of the tortoise and the hare, the essence is that slow but steady always wins over quick but careless. The moral of the story is that carelessness costs the race and the story provides the proof.

It is important that you maintain only one clear meta-message in each story. Stories with too many ideas and morals included are difficult to understand and draw a clear conclusion.

Ask yourself, what is the meta-message that I'm trying to communicate? Remember, meta-messages are big, compelling ideas people can believe in. What do I want people to walk away understanding about us and our products or services?

The meta-message is the place where you start developing your story. You create, position, and package the characters of your story to support it. Your narrative wraps around it so that when you tell the story the meta-message is implicit and understood. Understanding the meta-message sets up all future narrative subliminal persuasion tactics.

The Hook

Every powerful story must have a hook that pulls you in, that helps you identify with the central figure of the story, the protagonist.

The hook is a statement that the people hearing the story identify with or find shocking or that supports a belief they already have. The hook should leave them with an intense desire to know more.

Some of the hardest work you'll do on your story is developing the hook. Start by asking yourself this question, "What would people find shocking, or disturbing? Or, what would they find not surprising, or supportive of their existing beliefs about me, my product, service, or idea?"

I provided you an example of a good hook in Chapter 1 when I told you that the book I wanted to write was too dangerous for my publisher to publish, that it was too polarizing. When you find out about that book, it will likely be from some version of this hook:

> *Read the only persuasion book written by Dave Lakhani that was too dangerous for the largest publishers in the world. The secrets of persuasion and influence were so polarizing and controversial that it was turned down outright.*

That hook invokes curiosity, it makes you wonder what there is to learn that you aren't learning here (you'll have to wait and see; the book *will* come to print and will be like nothing you've ever experienced before).

Conflict and the Antagonist

For the story to be effective, there must be conflict in the form of some kind of shared antagonist (that is, The Man, the government, the devil, the Illuminati, taxes, grime, health care, the war). The antagonist presents a challenge that our hero must overcome.

It is important to develop an antagonist that everyone can recognize as having a shared enemy that allows the person experiencing the story to become a part of the story. The more that the person experiences himself as being a part of the story or relating to the story, the more seamlessly he accepts it.

The Revelation

As your story progresses, the hero of your story must experience a revelation. The revelation may come in the form of a discovery, an encounter with a benevolent teacher, or a literal revelation from some divine authority. The revelation exposes success secrets that everyone presumed were true but were reserved for a select few. Our hero, once in possession of the secrets, is willing to reveal them to you so that you can experience the same results he has.

When you are crafting your story, your revelation can have far-reaching implications, but it should explore no more than one major outcome. That outcome should be a major belief outcome.

For example:

In selling business opportunities by information marketing (direct marketing through the Internet, direct mail, direct response television, or direct selling MLM opportunities), offer a singular big promise for the riches you desperately crave and deserve.

Nearly all of the stories follow a very similar construct. They start out with the meta-message that you can, and in fact do, deserve to be rich. The story starts out with our hero telling you his story. "I was broke and struggling with no prospects of a better job when, by accident, sheer power of will, or divine intervention I discovered a process that virtually anyone can use to get rich and I want to do something no one else ever does: I want to share these secrets with you because I make all the money I need."

Layer On the Proof and Link It

We need to tell another critical piece of the story for the revelation to be accepted and compliance assured. This is the piece where we link us to them, we are alike, and we layer on proof that the revelation is true and that we truly were just like them. We link the idea that we used to do the same thing that they do now with the idea that the secrets we are about to reveal will transform them like they transformed us. Why? Because we are alike.

Let's continue with the previous example.

> It doesn't matter your level of income, your level of education, if you have special skills, or even where you live. I was living in a van down by the river (tip of the hat to the late and hilarious Chris Farley), I was working in a dead-end job that was stealing my life, I was working 80 hours a week and missing the most important part of my kid's life.

The storyteller simply chooses the part of the story that best matches the reality of his audience and layers it in. He then moves to the proof portion.

> And, best of all, because we are alike, these secrets will work for you, too, and the secrets will start working immediately. Look how they worked for these people (insert social proof/ testimonials here).

The story goes on to reveal some of the secrets so that you can see that they are real and exclusive. (For example, "The rich know banking secrets you don't; go to your bank and talk to them about their private banking programs.") It all sounds very logical, it follows a pattern that reinforces a belief that you have that you deserve to be rich and if you just had one lucky break you would be and this might be it.

The Conclusion

The conclusion is to bring the story to an emotionally compelling close. That close must include a call to action and the promise of a better future that the meta-message promises.

The conclusion also shows the student evolving into the teacher or the keeper of the secrets who benevolently shares them with those who are on the same path.

Let's finish the example that we began earlier.

> I know how you feel. Like all the people you've seen who've been successful using this system, you've tried everything. You've worked hard, paid your taxes, even tried other systems, but none of them have the time-tested and economy-proven techniques that I'm going to give you. You simply need to take action, call now, click here, invest the small fee that the course costs (because one of the secrets is that there is power in the transfer of money or they'd give it to you for free) and the secrets are yours and I'll see you in the hallowed halls of the rich reserved for us.

Now, I used a very obvious story that we've all heard a million times. And, chances are that you even bought into it a few times. But the truth of the subliminal persuasion that affected you was not the power of this story; it was the cumulative power of your exposure to the meta-message (you deserve to be and can be rich). What will determine the effectiveness of this story is how congruent the secrets are, and the product is with your personal experience. If they are congruent, you'll likely buy again. If you have any success, you'll become an ardent fan who spreads the story over and over again. And, if one of the profit points revolves around you spreading the story as an endorsing evangelist, you'll spread it with all your energy and soul.

Let's look at how the process might be used in a local accounting firm.

Meta-message: The IRS takes too much of my money and I want it back.

The Hook: Did you know that people who earned over $50,000 last year paid on average 25 percent more tax than they had to and their accountants never told them?

Conflict and the Antagonist: The Internal Revenue Service does not reward accountants for taking advantage of legal loopholes available to you. In fact, they go out of their way to hide them. And, accountants don't get paid more to find them for you. I grew up in a family that paid their taxes without question. They took basic deductions and nothing more. We got a modest refund back each year. I went to college and started studying accounting. I went back over my parents' tax returns for the last 10 years and discovered that they'd left almost $25,000 in the Internal Revenue Service's coffers, money that they could have used for a vacation, investments, even to pay for my schooling! I talked to them about it and they said exactly what people like you say to me, "No one told us."

I was outraged that my parents, upstanding people, hardworking, and kind, were paying an unfair amount of taxes because their accountant didn't want any extra scrutiny from the IRS. He just wanted to get as many returns done in the shortest time possible. There is virtually no incentive to an accountant to find deductions for you.

The Revelation: I began to study the tax code and the brightest minds in tax law and code interpretation. I discovered that there are literally dozens of loopholes that the average person can take advantage of if they know what to look for. I started with my parents and went back through their last three years of taxes and was able to file amended returns for all three years and the IRS had to write them a check for $5,200! That was an unexpected windfall. But I wanted to be sure. So I did my own taxes and those of family and friends just to be sure. In virtually every case, we got a refund. My folks called their old accountant and asked whether he thought they should look at their taxes for any missed deductions and he said, "We took every deduction you had coming that wouldn't send up a red flag to the IRS; any small amount wouldn't be worth the potential problem." I don't know about you, but I think that $5,200 is no small amount.

The Conclusion: I've developed a program that allows you to regain all of the taxes you have due for the past three years and I take all the risk. If I can't find at least a $1,000 refund for you in your past three years' taxes, you owe me nothing and we part ways as friends. But if I do, you'll pay my standard amended return filing fee of $150 per return. If I find you just $1,001 in savings, you still net $551 in your pocket. All you need to do is bring me your last three years' statements and I can get started right away. Your money belongs to you, not the IRS. Once you have your money back where it belongs, I'm going to ask you to be a client for life. Is that fair?

You see, by simply creating a narrative that leads them through a process that concludes in their favor, they've made the decision to buy long before you ask them to.

Subliminal Selling Secret

Develop an elevator pitch that combines the power of the question with narrative to create a qualifying statement that will literally instantly qualify or disqualify everyone you meet. Keep your meta-message in mind as you develop your pitch.

Start with the question or phrase: "Have you ever . . ." Add the qualifying statement: "Met someone who _____ or has seen the _____ of your dreams?

The answer to "Have you ever met someone who _____ " should be a *no* or a *yes* with a question. If they say no, you simply say that is exactly what I do; would you like to experience _____? If they say yes and they really have, then you know they are not a client or if you don't think they have, you simply ask them to tell you about that person so you can further determine whether they really have met someone like you before.

In the case of "Have you ever seen the _____ of your dreams?" whether they say yes or no, you say, "I'd love to hear about the _____ of your dreams because I have a unique process for helping people like you make that dream come true." Their next question, of course, will be, "How do you do that?" which is the invitation to begin your story.

Joel Bauer, author of *How To Persuade People Who Don't Want To Be Persuaded* (Wiley, 2004) is the master and originator of this technique and helped me refine and polish this technique to the point that it is nearly imperceptible when used. Thank you, Joel, you are masterful.

What does our accountant's elevator pitch sound like?

Prospect: Hi, I'm William Roberts, what do you do?

Accountant: Have you ever met someone who beats the IRS at its own game and gets you at least a $1,000 refund check from taxes you've already filed?

Prospect: No . . .

Accountant: That is exactly what I do. Would you like a refund check in the amount of at least $1,000 from the IRS in your hands in the next 60 days?

Prospect: Absolutely!

And that is the power of a well-constructed narrative to move someone who would normally have said no to beg for more information.

Implementation Is Everything

Money Follows Action

Put down this book before you go any further and deconstruct your current legend. Determine what the story is that people are taking away about you. Ask yourself the following questions:

- Is this the correct story that I want the masses to tell one another about me or my company?
- In what ways can the story be enhanced to create a much more congruent and emotional narrative that will move the masses?
- What is the meta-message of the story that is currently being told and does it need to be changed or improved?

Develop your 30-second elevator pitch that initiates your narrative interaction with your prospects.

Wouldn't you rather have people asking you for more information than having to sell to them all the time?

You are beginning to understand the power of Subliminal Persuasion.

ESSENTIAL FURTHER STUDY

Books

Storytelling: Branding In Practice—Klaus Fog, Christian Budtz, Baris Yakaboylu (Springer, 2005)

Brainwashing—Kathleen Taylor (Oxford, 2004)

How to Persuade People Who Don't Want to Be Persuaded—Joel Bauer and Mark Levy (Wiley, 2004)

Audio Interview

boldapproach.com/benmack: An interview with Ben Mack on creating a legend platform. This is a must-listen exposé on legendary branding.

Movies

Wag the Dog—(New Line Home Video, 1998)

4

Control the Emotion and the Content

The emotions aren't always immediately subject to reason,
but they are always immediately subject to action.

— James Joyce

Emotions nearly always play a significant role in achieving persuasion. In sales, it is often said that people buy emotionally and justify rationally.

One of the biggest mistakes that I see people making that causes resistance to persuasion or outright failure of the attempt is the misunderstanding of emotions and emotional content.

One of my most vivid memories of an in-home sales presentation was for Vulcan fire alarms. I'm not even sure if they are still in existence. But I'll never forget the salesman who came to sell the alarm.

The salesman arrived and began to explain the value of having fire alarms. When we decided not to buy, he attempted to engage our emotions. He said to my mom, "Imagine how you'll feel looking at the burned dead bodies of your sons knowing that for just a few dollars a month, you could have saved their lives."

Rather than being emotionally overcome, my mom just laughed and said, "I can promise you, if my sons die in a house fire I'm in, I won't be alive to see their dead bodies; I'll have perished trying to get them out." In one sentence, my mom defeated his "closes 'em every time" technique for harnessing emotion.

Emotions by their very definition are feelings that spring outward in response to some stimulus. To be subliminally persuasive, you must understand which emotions you are appealing to and attempting to get a reaction from.

The pressure of having to pay for fire detectors with money we didn't have evoked a much stronger emotional reaction in my mom than an idea that seemed highly unlikely to her, that someone in the house wouldn't wake up and get everyone out in the event of a fire. The salesman also activated a second emotion in my mom, which was the feeling of being disrespected by assuming that she'd fall for such an obvious ploy.

The key emotions that most persuaders should concern themselves with are:

Desire—A sense of intense want or a feeling of identifying what is missing and wanting that.

Lust—An intense desire or craving for something (including sex). It is often not physically tangible, like power.

Loss—The anticipation of not having something that they could or already have.

Shame—A feeling of doing something dishonorable. In the case of sales, marketing, and persuasion, the emotion of shame is often associated with not taking action when you know you should. For example, forgoing health insurance to buy a new car.

Pleasure—Pleasure is not technically an emotion, but rather a grouping of emotions to create an experience referred to as pleasure. It includes happiness, pride, and other subsets of emotions. The anticipation of good and desirable feelings from actions you take or things you acquire.

Anticipated Pain—Pain is often incorrectly referred to as an emotion. According to Dr. Antonio Damasio, "Pain is the perception of a sensory representation of local living-tissue dysfunction. . . . In other words, the organism is designed to respond to the actual or threatened loss of integrity of its tissue with a particular type of signaling." Anticipation of pain is one of the most powerful emotional sets that you can leverage. It is the self-inflicted feeling of what an experience will be like for the person if something within her control occurs because she doesn't take an action. It is also often a very visceral reaction to a problem she is currently experiencing.

Fear—Forms a persuasion perspective closely associated with loss. It is a sense of a lack of safety or anticipation of loss.

Flattery—A feeling of being somehow special and desirable.

Pity—This is most often induced to raise funds for charities, and so forth. It is a transposition of a very unfortunate person or incident on to yourself and feeling how you imagine you'd feel in a similar situation, and wanting to make a difference now.

Consequences—Cause and effect. It is the sense of what could happen by not taking action or not making a decision.

Status or Celebrity—Keeping up with the Joneses, a positive feeling of being on display or receiving very positive attention for some action. This is one of the most overlooked emotions by professional persuaders. Many people want their 15 minutes of fame so they can leverage it . . . or at least enjoy it.

Approval—A feeling of making a right decision or doing the right thing and receiving positive recognition for it.

Love—Advertising has done a very good job of linking the feeling of love with products, particularly food. A sense of well-being, connectedness, and unconditional acceptance.

Hate—Virulent dislike, revulsion. A very effective emotion to evoke when making comparisons or setting up us-versus-them scenarios.

To create an emotional reaction to your message, you must create a powerful appeal that encourages people to feel the correct emotion. Overt appeals are rarely as effective as subliminal appeals. In the case of the Vulcan salesman, his appeal was so overt, that, for my mom, it had virtually no impact.

Many of the techniques we've already explored precondition, or set up, the appeal, and any interaction has the person already feeling a certain emotion. Persuasion occurs when you fulfill the emotional desire that your efforts have created.

SETTING UP THE APPEAL

You must know what emotions you are hoping to engage so you can properly set up an appeal. It is imperative that you understand generally what your audience will respond to or is seeking.

One of the best ways to effectively set up an appeal is through effective questioning, getting people to express what it is that they desire most. But that isn't the end; you need to ask questions around what is important about that desire. Once you know what is important to the person or the group, you can then set up the emotional appeal.

Let's look at my three-year-old daughter as an example. I was recently shopping for some educational toys that would help her learn better or more efficiently. I particularly wanted things that would help her begin to learn to see patterns, something I was not taught in my youth.

The store clerk greeted me and asked me what I was looking for. I told him that I was looking for toys for my daughter that would help her learn more about pattern recognition. He proceeded to show me several toys and suggested that the best toy was one of the most expensive. He went on to talk to me about the quality of the toy and the research that went into it. Those were important things to me, but not the most important. Had he received the education you are receiving right now, he might have asked a series of questions that would have gone something like this:

Salesman: Welcome to My Toy Store, is there something specific you are looking for?

Me: Yes, educational toys that help children learn pattern recognition.

Salesman: Let me show you what we have. What is important in learning pattern recognition for you?

Me: I believe that it allows children to learn more easily when they are able to recognize the patterns in language and math and so forth.

Salesman: Interesting. . . . Did you learn pattern recognition when you were young?

Me: No, education was not a priority when I was a child, so no one really taught me how to learn (strong emotional content around loss and shame). But all the really smart people I know (emotional content around acceptance by a certain group of people) understand how to recognize and interpret patterns in information and their surroundings, so I learned later in life (emotional content around pride).

Salesman: We have a wide variety of toys that help children learn patterns, but the ones that are recommended by some of the top learning institutions like Harvard will help your child have the advantage you didn't much earlier. Is earlier mastery important to you? (Encouraging me to engage my emotional content around wanting my daughter to be smart and not feel the same shame I did around what I perceived as a deficient education.)

Me: Absolutely!

Salesman: Wonderful. These are the top two toys for early mastery. Why don't we let your daughter look at them with you and see which ones appeal more to her? (Encourages me to get involved in the teaching, learning, and selection process with my daughter, firing off many emotions around being connecting, loving, and so forth.)

Me: Perfect.

Salesman: It looks like she likes this one the best. Is there anything else you need in addition to this toy? It is wonderful
to see you taking an active role in your daughter's learning. So many people don't and children are left to learn on
their own. (Testing to be sure that the emotional content
was correct and validating my beliefs.) It must feel terrific
to be able to give your daughter this gift of advancement
early in life. (Reflecting my emotional content.) I can only
imagine how wonderful it will feel for you to see her graduate from a top college and be able to look back and know
that little decisions like this one set the course of her life in
ways yours couldn't have been.

Here are the steps for setting up emotional appeal:

1. Identify the emotions you are appealing to.
2. Create vivid word pictures that point to the emotions.
3. Ask powerful questions that get the audience to put
   themselves in the picture and experience what they are
   or would be feeling. Questions are your secret weapon to
   leading people into an experience.
4. Suggest what they are feeling and acknowledge it.
5. Encourage them to feel more of that emotion, and if it
   is an emotion they'd like less of, link to your product,
   service, or idea and demonstrate how it will lessen the
   feeling.

When your audience is in an emotional state, they are not
focused on critical thinking; they are caught up in the feelings
that the emotions create.

Words contain great emotional content. By choosing your words carefully, you can create very powerful emotional connectedness. All too often, persuaders fall in love with the language that is comfortable for them to use, not the representational language of their clients.

One of the best places to begin learning more about your clients is online. There are tremendous resources now available where people actively share their thoughts, emotions, and even personal content. Start out by looking at social networking sites like Facebook.com, Linkedin.com, Tbd.com, and Multiply.com.

These sites are chock full of great information, typically in people's own words about how they think, consider, emote, and feel. They give you tremendous insight into the markets you hope to influence. Go one step deeper, look at the groups that form around your focus area on those sites and actively peruse the content. When you begin to consume this information, you'll begin to see commonalities, hot buttons, and emotional content that you can leverage to be seen as a savior, or at minimum, a realistic solution in the market.

Watching blogs that focus on your industry is another great way to understand the emotion of your market. Read what impassioned writers are talking about so that you can carefully craft your message to reach the market.

You should also study the media releases of your competitors and others in noncompetitive companies in the same market. Understand what emotional message they are sending your market. Once you understand the emotions that your competitors focus on, you can make a determination as to their effectiveness. You may find many openings that you can exploit in your competition just by listening to what they are saying and comparing it with the emotional content of your audience.

Subliminal Selling Secret

Craft your story to include the dominant emotions that your clients are likely to be experiencing and show them how you overcame the challenge that initiated the emotion.

You can lead with the emotion in ads or even in person. Your word pictures can create the sense of the emotion they are feeling while either heightening it or leading them to a solution.

The more engaged in the emotion you get the audience, the more likely they are to accept your presentation of support of their emotions or in supporting them to move past the emotions they are currently feeling.

You may use a combination of graphics and words expressing emotional content in print and television ads. In radio, it can be done with words and voice inflection. Work on making every statement emotionally impactful and your persuasiveness will increase dramatically.

RITUALS AND EMOTIONS

Rituals are highly emotionally charged events. One of the fastest ways to engage emotion is to center the ritual around your product or service . . . and if you can't identify one, create it.

The drink absinthe was outlawed in the early years of the twentieth century in many parts of Europe, and in the United States in 1912. Even during the period of illegality, absinthe maintained a cultlike following for its apparent ability to create extreme creativity in some people (Vincent van Gogh, Edgar

Allan Poe, and Ernest Hemingway were absinthe drinkers). One of the big appeals in addition to the purported hallucinogenic effect of absinthe was the ritual of drinking it. Absinthe was dropped one drop at a time through a sugar cube into a glass before being served. The waiting created anticipation for the effect. There is a sense of doing something forbidden for people who still drink it. Absinthe is no longer outlawed in the United States and has a very significant cult following, even though it has been declared safe and not a hallucinogen.

When you identify emotions that people are feeling and begin to predict correctly what will happen next, it usually will. This is a version of the placebo effect.

Most people have buying rituals that they follow and those rituals lead to an experience of feeling confident and making a purchase or not feeling confident and avoiding the purchase. These rituals are highly charged emotionally. If you understand the ritual, you are able to help them recreate it and activate positive persuasive compliance emotions. You can also use it to set up an us-versus-them situation with your competitors. In the us-versus-them scenario, you demonstrate and have them go through the positive buying ritual and point out which emotional pieces are missing in your competitor's business. Rituals are highly subliminally persuasive because there is a presumption of an outcome implicit in participating in a ritual.

Pay particular attention to the processes that people go through in advance of buying your products and services. Once you've identified their ritual, engage them in it earlier. The sooner you engage their emotions, the faster persuasive compliance occurs. Here is an example of how understanding a ritual can become highly persuasive.

One ritual for buying for a large subset of buyers is getting a good deal. They enter the store and search through rack after rack of merchandise looking for hidden bargains and celebrate their successes with their friends. So the ritual is: Go to the store, look through many items, find the best deals, celebrate with friends.

If you know that this particular subset of buyers is important to your business, you may identify them and mark them out. You may create an event that allows them to come in early one or two days a month so they and another small group like them are in the store. Everyone is going through a very similar ritual and they are bonded because they were selected to be there, based on their ritual and their label (savvy shopper, frugal shopper, and so forth). The result is that they tell all their friends who are like them to come to the store with them in times that they are not invited in for the special day in hopes that their friends, too, will be selected.

Let me give you another example. In the early 1990s, I owned one of the nation's first used-personal-computers-only stores. I sold large volumes of PCs and associated components. I was very focused on getting in used equipment, bagging it in static bags and putting it in bins on the shelves so that it could be easily found by me and customers. One day, I got in late and a shipment of used parts and components had arrived. Because of the uniqueness of the store, it was not uncommon to have a line of people waiting at the door when I opened. This day was no exception. I couldn't get everything put away before

I opened and there was too much to put it all in the back. So, with no choice, I let people in and they went absolutely crazy. They dug through boxes with great intensity looking for exactly what they wanted. Nothing was priced, so they were offering me what they thought was fair for the products and to my shock it was nearly always at least 25 percent more then I'd have charged for it, and often double.

I realized in that moment that there was a buying ritual that I had missed . . . actually I'd seen it repeated dozens of times at garage sales and auctions, but I assumed that it wouldn't apply to my business. Boy, was I wrong. From that moment on, everything went in boxes, on the floor, and on the shelves; there were no prices in most cases, and the lines and crowds got bigger, and I sold nearly three times as much the year I discovered the ritual as the year before.

What was interesting was the number of people who eagerly and happily brought their friends to shop with them, people who were just like them. People who purchased a lot of products.

All of those customers shared many similar emotions: elation at finding a good deal, fear of losing out on a good deal, pride in finding one, lust for the most expensive computers in the store, and a very real sense of loss when they missed a deal, which was buoyed by a fierce determination not to let it happen again.

Based on observing the most ardent participants of the ritual, I was able to sell an early morning membership whereby once a week when my main new stock came in, people who spent the most with me got to come in half an hour before anyone else. Those people were willing to pay $250 a year to be able to participate.

Shared Emotions Bond People

Groups most often exhibit shared emotions. If you want to persuade the masses more effectively, you simply present them with an opportunity to share their emotions with others who feel the same way. One of the most powerful subliminal persuasion tools you can use is the creation of a group with shared ideas and emotional commitments and attachments. You don't have to do a lot of work once the group is formed; you simply need to persuade the influencers and leaders in the group and present them with the ideas you want them to promote or support, and they will.

People who are truly emotionally engaged are typically much more capable of raising the emotional level of an event than someone from the front of the room who has less emotional intensity or commitment. Simply direct the emotional content of the group to reap the benefit and implant your idea or message or to gain persuasive compliance.

Focus on emotions. The person most in control of the emotions of the audience owns them.

Implementation Is Everything

Money Follows Action

Before you go any further in this book, I want you to ask yourself the following questions:

- What is the dominant emotion that my audience must feel for them to make a decision or accept my idea?
- What emotions are they experiencing when they initially engage with me?

(continued)

(continued)

- What rituals does my audience go through in the buying or acceptance process?
- What patterns of behavior do they demonstrate during their buying process?
- What is the most important thing I can do to appeal to the dominant emotion they need to feel to accept my idea or make a decision?
- How do I preemptively engage a feeling of negative emotions related to the processes of my competitors?

Work on developing a question set that you can use in your one-on-one persuasive endeavors or power questions that lead to emotion and link to you, your products, or ideas in your ads.

ESSENTIAL FURTHER STUDY

Books

The Feeling of What Happens—Antonio Damasio (Harcourt, 1999)

Ritual Theory, Ritual Practice—Catherine Bell (Oxford, 1992)

The Stuff of Thought—Steven Pinker (Viking, 2007)

Audio Interview

discoverthecode.com: interview with Clotaire Rapaille on the culture code and emotional imprints as they relate to product decision processes.

5

GET A REAL ENDORSEMENT

People may like a particular piece of music, but then the additional testimonial that goes along with it from others can do a lot to help that decision.

—Psychologist Terry Pettijohn

Just about everyone who has studied persuasion for any period of time has heard of Social Proof. For those who haven't, social proof simply says that we are more likely to do something that we see others doing. When social proof (someone else doing it) exists, our decision is much easier. Everyone likes making good decisions; fewer people like to be the first person to try something. We even have great sayings that support not going first: "You can always tell the pioneers; they are the ones with the arrows in their backs."

Getting others to endorse your work, your ideas, your business, or you personally is another example of social proof. The most effective persuaders today all make very liberal use of very powerful testimonials.

The biggest argument I hear for not having and using powerful testimonials is that people don't understand how to get endorsements from people who might be able to offer them great credibility in the eyes of their target audience. Those who often do get a testimonial don't get a testimonial that is really usable for their persuasion endeavor.

Social proof is a very powerful subliminal persuader because even if people recognize the overt attempt at compliance that a testimonial makes, they are moved by the person giving the testimonial. This is increasingly true the higher the stature of the person delivering the testimonial. When persuading the masses, the key is to have a good number of well-developed testimonials that span a number of personality styles and backgrounds. Your testimonials should also include a good mix of men and women so as to appeal to everyone.

Endorsements by organizations or heads of organizations carry additional persuasive power. When an endorsement comes from a company or company head, you are getting not only the endorsement of the person who gives it, but the transfer of power and credibility from the organization itself. When faced with a conflict about whether to assign credibility or trust to an endorsement, the audience will often fall back on the idea that "ten thousand people who are part of this organization can't be wrong." There is a belief that a company or group like them wouldn't endorse something that isn't good for them.

THE COMPONENTS OF A SUBLIMINALLY PERSUASIVE ENDORSEMENT

1. The endorser should have high credibility, either as a user of your product or adopter of your idea.
2. The endorser should have high credibility with your audience or a subsection of that audience.
3. The content of the endorsement should be clearly focused on one or two ideas at most. It should consist of demonstrations of how the product, service, or idea has been used and the specific results of the use.
4. If in writing or audio, the endorsement must clearly identify who the person is who is giving the endorsement. Endorsements are most effective in the following order:

   - Live and in person
   - Video
   - Audio
   - Read by a supportive third party
   - Written

In an age of technology, it is becoming easier and easier to get live endorsements and video endorsements. Be sure to collect as many as you can.

It is important that you do not assume that endorsers understand how to endorse you properly. To create the most impactful endorsement, you should feel very comfortable asking for specifically what you need from them and even directing them to the extent necessary to get the outcome you need.

You should always have a means of collecting an available endorsement whenever you are working with people who may be in a position to give you one. The tool I find most convenient is the Canon Powershot SD series camera. The Canon SD1000 is the latest and best in the series as I put these words to paper. It allows you to record 30 to 60 fps (frames per second) video with the touch of a button. What makes this my preferred tool for collecting endorsements is that it captures digital video, which I can then edit with simple video editing software, which allows me to put the person's name on the video and include any other information I want. It also allows me to rip the audio out of the video and use that in other applications, like radio ads, for example.

When you present an endorsement in two modalities, for example, video and later in audio, an impression of that person is created as having had a lot more to say and feels even more strongly about your offering. One of the things that I do regularly when I have only a written endorsement is to display a photo of the person who gave the testimonial along with the text and ask a third party to read the endorsement. Most people will quickly forget that the person reading the endorsement is not the person who wrote it and you also assume all the power and credibility that the person reading has with the group.

CONNECTING WITH THE PEOPLE WHO CAN ENDORSE YOU

There are three groups of people who can and will endorse you.

1. People who use your products and services
2. People who know you and like you

3. People who don't know you but who see value in what you are providing

In the case of people who use your products and services, it really is as simple as asking them to share their experience and then shaping their story to fit your needs.

The best way to get the endorsement is to tell the person that you need their endorsement and ask them to provide it. It is always best to coach them through exactly what it is that you need them to say for the endorsement to be most effective. Most people willing to endorse you are also willing to take some direction. The important keys are to get them to say the most supportive things about your product and to use the most emotionally evocative language possible. It is often easy to couch your criticism and coaching in questions. By simply asking something like, "Did you mean ———— when you said ————?" Their answer will often be yes, and you can then say, "Do you think it would be easier for a layman to understand what you said if you said ————; would you mind?" By taking the approach of asking questions, it doesn't seem as if you are being critical and it allows you to get what you need.

Not having to pay money for endorsements is the ideal situation, because paid endorsements in most cases need to be revealed. You can, however, give the endorsers special access, preferred service, and so forth, as a result of their endorsement and even to position them to give you the endorsement. Targeting people you hope to induce to provide an endorsement with a higher level of service or with special incentives is a very powerful technique. The only downside is that you condition those people to expect to always be treated in a preferential way.

You need to be sure that the continued level of treatment is justified by the endorsement.

People who know and like you are also great candidates for very powerful endorsements. They are, in many ways, superior candidates, because they will say whatever you need them to say and they will often be reflecting their care and concern for you as much as their commitment to your offering, and that care and concern for you will often come across as a deep commitment to the offering.

Because of the flexibility of the people who know you and like you, you can many times get action endorsements, that is, endorsements of them actually using your product. These kinds of endorsements are incredibly persuasive, because they allow people to actually see what the person is describing and they can put themselves in the picture and easily imagine a similar result.

The great news about the first two groups is that you hopefully don't have to look very far to find them. The third group presents a slightly more difficult challenge for some people but it needn't.

There are many people who don't know you but who will see value in what you do and who will endorse you because of it. These endorsements can be straightforward and free. For example, I don't pay for the endorsements of my book; even from people I don't know but whose work I respect and who are well recognized. Endorsements can also be paid endorsements. This is most often seen in consumer goods, particularly when creating influence strategies for hard-to-reach groups like teens or senior citizens, who tend to be more skeptical.

There is an old belief that we are separated from any other person on earth by only six others, and by leveraging those connections, we can get connected with anyone. One of the major weekly news shows did a live experiment with the idea and proved that it actually did work . . . with regular people as well as with people whom you wouldn't expect, for example, a random kid in New York.

The point for our purpose is not whether you can reach someone in six connections but whether you will reach out and ask for the endorsement. I was speaking with Ben Mack, author of *Think Two Products Ahead* (Wiley, 2007) while writing this chapter. Ben is exceptional at connecting with people he'd seemingly have no business connecting with, and getting them to promote him and endorse him in all kinds of ways. When I asked him how he did it, his initial answer was simple; he said, "I just call them and ask them." But as I dug deeper, I found that he had a very specific strategy for getting people to say yes to him. First, he got to know something about the person. He researched them online, read their work, became familiar with their beliefs. Then, he looked for a connection, someone who could introduce him either directly or who could introduce him to someone who could. He would then ask for the introduction. Once the introduction is made, Ben finds some commonalities and explores them. He rarely asks for anything up front; in fact, he is more curious about what he can do for the other person, curious to the extent that they often feel compelled (law of reciprocation) to offer to do something in return and that is when Ben strikes. But the one thing that I noticed that I think makes Ben more successful than others who have a similar process, is his intense interest in the person. He asks very penetrating questions to learn about him, his values, his beliefs, his passions . . . and he listens intensely to the answers. They have been subliminally persuaded without even knowing what they'll be saying yes to shortly.

It is truly amazing to me how many people say yes to Ben . . . and I'm confident you'll be just as amazed at how many people will say yes to you, too, if you follow Ben's strategy.

The key to getting the yes in asking for people who have high credibility but who do not know you is to present your request in a way that has reciprocal value. They need to see that by giving you their endorsement, there is something in it for them as well. It may be that their endorsement might make them visible to a new market or it might make them personally more visible. Never underestimate the power of exposure and perceived celebrity in getting agreements to give an endorsement.

When you get an endorsement from someone you don't know who doesn't use your product or service, it is important to help her completely understand what she is endorsing. If you can give her a sample, a trial, or an experience, it is even better, because she'll then be responding out of her own experience. If not, it is best to tell her the most important and powerful things that she might want to use or say in her endorsement. Like all of the other endorsers, it is important to coach her, but the time to do it is right up front, as you may not get a second shot at having her give you her endorsement. The key is to make the process as simple as possible for her with as little time commitment as necessary.

INDIRECT ENDORSEMENTS

Indirect endorsements are those endorsements that are implied endorsements. For example, if an athlete wears your custom-made hats, it is an implied endorsement by that person even if he doesn't endorse the product outright. While it is okay to identify who your customers are, you need to weigh the value of disclosing your customers to gain an indirect endorsement compared to having the person as a customer.

There are many other forms of indirect endorsement, and they include:

- *Sponsorships*—When you sponsor an event, the organizers feel compelled to endorse you. While this seems transparent as an attempt to persuade, it also creates a bond of sorts with the true believers at the event.
- *Product reviews*—Independent product reviews, when positive, are an indirect endorsement of the reviewer and the outlet it was reviewed for.
- *Donations*—Donation of products or services that are given away by credible third parties, for example, a charity. These giveaways often result in a planned or spontaneous endorsement of the product. This is also a great time to ask for an outright endorsement from someone you don't know who has high credibility.
- *Acceptance of products or services by social organizations or charities*—Be sure that you understand how you can use their name before you leverage the indirect endorsement.
- *Street teams and paid endorsers working events*—This is becoming more and more common. The pretty girl who recommends a particular CD or movie very well may be a paid endorser even though she appears to be an unbiased person just making a friendly recommendation. One company that has created a huge base of endorsers

who are not paid cash but who can earn perks, gifts, and so on, is Bzzagent.com. They specialize in creating word-of-mouth marketing by getting their "agents" (you can be one, too) to review and endorse your product or service. Agents earn points by the kinds of endorsements that they give and where.

There are many other forms of, and ways to get, indirect endorsements. The key is to spend some time thinking creatively about how you can get a third party to expose your offering to her audience in a way that appears that she is endorsing it.

Product placement is also another form of indirect endorsement that can have a great impact. Placement becomes more and more effective, depending on how well used and integrated the product becomes in the movie, television program, book, play, or other public performance. If you remember the reality television show hosted by Donald Trump called "The Apprentice," you saw that a regular fixture was a Marquis Jet. Trump's properties were regularly placed in the show along with his events. These kinds of placement imply an endorsement of the company being showcased.

When products move into the background in a public presentation like a movie or television show they can still have a tremendous impact. People who see the performance and later see the product may recall that they first saw it in a program that they really enjoyed and attribute to it a certain kind of respect or acceptance that in a moment of ambiguity would cause you to be the clear winner. There is also the added benefit of them not consciously recalling the product but having a sense or feeling that they've experienced it before in a way that was positive. One of the most effective companies specializing in product placement for persuaders is Hero Product Placement (heroprod uctplacement.com). Visit their site to learn more about the dynamics of product placement.

Whenever I promote a new book, I always send a copy to the CEOs of the Fortune 100, not because I think they'll read it but because many of their managers and gatekeepers will see the personally inscribed book and assume that if the boss is reading it, they should be, too. I'll be adding key business organizations to the mailing for this book because it is effective.

The more time you spend gathering direct and indirect endorsements, the more you will sell. Endorsements are highly subliminally persuasive because they come from trusted sources or appear in trusted places. The result is that when faced with a decision between a product or service offered by someone the buyer doesn't know, he'll most often make the decision to go with the product that is endorsed by someone like himself. If there isn't someone like the buyer doing the endorsing, then a product that seems to be endorsed by a person or company that is trusted is the second best choice.

There is no real reason to actively sell your products when you can let your endorsements do much of the selling for you.

Implementation Is Everything
Money Follows Action
Before you read the next chapter, take the following actions:

- List three customers that you should get an endorsement from right now.

(continued)

(continued)

- List at least three people you know and have a personal relationship with who could and will endorse you, your product, or your service.
- Make a list of your top 10 targets for endorsements by people you don't know but who have high credibility. Begin studying those people and making connections to get an introduction to them.

ESSENTIAL FURTHER STUDY

Books

Never Eat Alone—Keith Ferrazzi (Currency, 2005)
Applebee's America—Douglas Sosnik, Matthew Dowd, and Ron Fournier (Simon & Schuster, 2006)

Movies

Any James Bond movie (count the number of placements)
Transformers movie (Dreamworks, 2007)

6

UNDERSTAND BELIEFS AND TRUE BELIEVERS

The human brain is a complex organ with the wonderful power of enabling man to find reasons for continuing to believe whatever it is that he wants to believe.

—Voltaire

I can believe anything provided it is incredible.

—Oscar Wilde

For persuasion to be effective in the long term, a primary goal becomes moving people from being convinced to being ardent believers. The goal is to create converts who will not only change their way of thinking but who will actively seek to instill their beliefs on those around them. True believers are the persuader's version of the Christian church's evangelist.

They have a mission to share their beliefs with those who indicate the slightest interest or who demonstrate a chink in their own belief system. True believers remain true often in spite of evidence that their beliefs are no longer true. The fine line for the ethical persuasionist is to help the true believers evolve their beliefs as appropriate and when appropriate.

PROGRAMMING

In his remarkable book, *The Pig Who Sang to the Moon: The Emotional World of Farm Animals,* Jeffrey Moussaieff Masson wrote about a particular group of women who worked with cattle headed for slaughter. Masson asked these women about the doomed cows' feelings. "They don't have any," the women all agreed. "They are always the same, they feel nothing."

"At that moment," wrote Masson, "we all heard a loud bellowing. I asked why the cows were making that noise." The women shrugged it off as "nothing," explaining that cows that were separated from their calves were calling them. "The calves are afraid," one woman said, "and are calling for their mothers, and their mothers are afraid for their calves and are calling them, trying to reassure them."

"It sounded to me," Masson stated, "as if these people were suffering from . . . *confirmation bias,* which involves taking into account only evidence that confirms a belief already held and ignoring or dismissing evidence that disproves that same belief."

Think about that. Even the evidence of their own senses could not persuade them to alter an existing belief. "Programming leads to belief," says Richard F. Taflinger, a professor at the Edward R. Murrow School of Communication at Washington

State University. "What a person is programmed to believe is what that person does believe."

Subliminal Selling Secret

If you want to deeply influence an audience quickly and subliminally, you must understand what their core beliefs are. It doesn't matter what you are selling or what people are buying. When you understand their core, programmed beliefs, you are better able to adjust your story to fit their version of reality. It is much easier to sell to people by speaking to their beliefs rather than by confronting them or asking them to change.

If you need people to move their beliefs so you may gain persuasive compliance, you meet them at their current beliefs and you evolve the belief; you don't challenge it.

If I want someone to start eating organic food, I don't tell him that the food he currently eats is bad for him. I start with a premise and a belief that he likely has. That belief is that food tastes different today from when we were kids. By simply starting with a belief that we can both agree on, I can build a logic chain that will shift the belief from that point and move him to believe that organics taste better.

Once you've evolved the belief, you must present your audience with more examples of their new truth being correct over time or they may revert to their older, more ingrained belief when confronted by friends who want to go to McDonald's. If you are McDonald's, you understand the conversion to the new belief and you offer healthier choices so your customers can still enjoy their time with friends or eat better when they are in a hurry. You can also charge a little more for the convenience of a healthy meal, which reinforces another belief that most Americans have, which is that while you pay more for quality, it is worth it.

As a word, *programming* has only a slightly better reputation than *propaganda*.

Humans behave in accordance with how they perceive their surroundings. They perceive their surroundings in accordance with how they've been taught. How they've been taught (read: *programmed*) helps to cultivate beliefs. No one is more effective with this style of programming than McDonald's.

The news about McDonald's "branding" broke in the summer of 2007. A study showed that young children preferred food—*any* food, in fact—that came in a McDonald's wrapper. Identical foods were served in both name brand and unmarked wrappers and the children were asked which tasted better. The food adorned with the infamous Golden Arches won each and every time. Even a traditionally hated veggie like carrots tasted better to the kids when served in a McDonald's wrapper. "You see a McDonald's label and kids start salivating," said childhood development specialist Diane Levin.

"Advertisers have tried to do exactly what this study is talking about—to brand younger and younger children, to instill in them an almost obsessional desire for a particular brand-name product," said Dr. Victor Strasburger of the American Academy of Pediatrics. Dr. Tom Robinson, the study's author, said the kids' taste perception was "physically altered by the branding."

BELIEF AS SURVIVAL

If we were to evaluate our deeply held beliefs, we might discover that even if we're unsure why we hold these beliefs, we're convinced they must be defended at all costs. "In its simplest form, belief occurs as a mental act, a thinking process in the brain," writes Jim Walker of the No Beliefs web site. "To *believe* requires a conscious thought accepted as having some *truth* value. To communicate this thought requires spoken or written language. Not only does belief require thought, but also a mental feeling of *truth,* which, according to neurological brain research, occurs from the limbic part of the brain. Thus, belief occurs as a thought with a truth-value feeling attached."

Gregory W. Lester is a psychologist on the graduate faculty of the University of St. Thomas in Houston. "Belief," he explains, "is the name we give to the survival tool of the brain that is designed to augment and enhance the danger-identification function of our senses." To bring this concept into everyday life, think about your car parked in the driveway—as you sit in your living room unable to see the car. If your brain relied solely on current sensory data, you could not be sure where your car is. But instead, your brain calls upon what Lester calls its "internal map" of the location of your car. Therefore, contrary to immediate sensory evidence, you can comfortably own the *belief* that your car is in the driveway.

"This means that beliefs are designed to operate independent of sensory data," adds Lester. "As far as our brain is concerned, there is absolutely no need for data and belief to agree. They have each evolved to augment and supplement one another by contacting different sections of the world. They are designed to be able to disagree. The brain doesn't care whether or not the belief matches the data. It cares whether the belief is helpful for survival. Period."

Like many aspects of human psychology and neurology, the origin of our beliefs is a topic up for grabs. As research progresses, some patterns are being discovered but, in general, there are far, far more questions than answers.

"There's no doubt that there's a rich, complex human nature," says Noam Chomsky, a noted social commentator and a pioneer in modern cognitive study. "When you get to cultural patterns, belief systems, and the like, the guess of the next guy you meet at the bus stop is about as good as that of the best scientist. Nobody knows anything."

This sure hasn't stopped humans from trying to figure it all out.

THE BIOLOGY OF BELIEF

"Beliefs are among the most primitive and central of mental constructs, and yet there is little agreement as to what they are or how they should be construed," says Professor David J. Schneider of Rice University. "They are basic to our understanding of a wide range of central phenomena in modern psychology. For example, our beliefs are key components of our personalities and senses of identity, and our expressions of beliefs often define us to others. . . . Many of our behaviors, mundane and consequential, are affected by what we believe."

In his book, *The Biology of Belief: Unleashing The Power of Consciousness, Matter, and Miracles,* cell biologist Bruce H. Lipton states that thoughts "directly influence how the physical brain controls the body's physiology. Thought 'energy' can activate or inhibit the cell's function-producing proteins. . . . The fact is that harnessing the power of your mind can be more effective than the drugs you have been programmed to believe you need."

Perhaps the most common proof of Lipton's hypothesis is what we call the *placebo effect* (for example, "The beneficial effect in a patient following a particular treatment that arises from the patient's expectations concerning the treatment rather than from the treatment itself").

"The critical factor," says Irving Kirsch, a psychologist at the University of Connecticut, "is our beliefs about what's going to happen to us. You don't have to rely on drugs to see profound transformation."

While cognitive science and the study of the human brain is—as previously mentioned—an ever-changing, evolving, and relatively new field, current research seems to support the claim that a person's beliefs, sensory experience, and thoughts can affect neurochemistry—and thus affect outcomes.

Consider the concept of hypnosis. Neuropsychologists point to alterations in brain activity to explain this phenomenon. EEG research shows a shift in the location of brain activity during the hypnotic process. Hence, the neurological changes just may help facilitate the power of suggestion.

While not exactly an accepted scientific term, the "power of suggestion" is a confirmed psychological mechanism. Our subconscious can accept or reject input. From repressed childhood memories to self-help mantras, the input varies widely, but what the subconscious accepts is what it responds to and thus acts on. (As any advertiser or marketer knows, the power of suggestion can be augmented through repetition.)

What all this suggests is that despite the ballyhoo surrounding genetic research and the mapping of the human genome, we humans are made up of much more than our DNA. "We are *not* the expression of our genes," declares Ruth Hubbard, professor emeritus of biology at Harvard, "and knowing their location on the chromosomes, or their composition, does not enable someone to predict what we will look or be like. . . . It is a mistake to put too much weight on genes or DNA."

It is also a mistake to believe we can accurately predict the unpredictable.

"Don't assume that people who commit atrocities are atrocious people, or people who do heroic things are heroic," declares Professor Lee Ross of Stanford. "Don't get overly carried away; don't think, because you observed someone under one set of discrete situational factors, that you know what they're like, and therefore can predict what they would do in a very different set of circumstances." Under the right circumstances, says Ross, people could be led to do "terrifically altruistic and self-sacrificing things that we would never have agreed to before we started."

Possible Lesson: Beliefs, opinions, and behaviors are more adaptable than many of us realize and hence are almost always subject to change from situation to situation.

EVIDENCE

When asked what he'd want people to believe if it were up to him, renowned British biologist Richard Dawkins replied, "I would want them to believe whatever evidence leads them to; I would want them to look at the evidence, judge it on its merits, not accept things because of internal revelation or faith, but purely on the basis of evidence."

But what happens when evidence is doled out on a need-to-know basis?

Many people are concerned about the effects global warming and climate change, but that concern is often outweighed, for example, by the belief that we cannot live without an automobile. This is not a coincidence. Carmakers continue to spend billions to keep this powerful belief alive. Consider Chevrolet.

Despite the fact that automobiles create nearly 1.5 billion tons of carbon dioxide each year, Chevy gained prestige and notoriety for co-sponsoring the Live Earth web page. To take things further, according to the carmaker's latest promotional campaign, Chevy is "an American Revolution" (that is, something radically new and exciting). The newsletter Chevy sends to its dealer is, in fact, named *Revolution*. And while the carmakers continue to spend money to keep beliefs alive that support their economic reality, they are moving people in the direction of other fuels as they introduce multifuel and alternative fuel cars while sponsoring events that spotlight what can be done. They are creating new beliefs and new believers by meeting people where they are and aligning with the thought leaders in their new market. They are also doing something else that is very subliminally persuasive: They are providing significant financial support for groups that need it and even if they are demonized for what might be seen as their complicity in the problem, they are defended by the thought leaders preemptively so as to maintain their funding. The requirement is not to influence the masses; it is to influence the decision makers and allow them to spin the financial commitment in a way that can be easily accepted by the true believers.

Both the automobile and the lifestyle it inspires have risen to prominence through the power of relentless suggestion and the development of associated beliefs. We no longer consciously acknowledge the presence of cars on the street, the highway, and in driveways from coast to coast and the myriad forms of *carchitecture:* the countless structures that exist exclusively to nourish and support the car culture, for example, the highway, on-ramp, off-ramp, gas station, strip mall, car wash, auto repair shop, car rental establishment, bridges, tunnels, and, of course, the suburbs. This is all the result of a very powerful belief structure carefully crafted and tough to change.

It's simply expected that singers will sing about cars, writers will write about cars, actors will act in cars, and practically everyone will become a motorist. Even environmental activists regularly drive to their protests and rallies. Owning a car is now considered a virtual birthright, an actuality not open for debate on any philosophical level. As a result, although cars have been around for a relatively short time, the culture that facilitates their subconscious acceptance has quickly passed the point of any widespread scrutiny. Yes, we own a car (or SUV) and yes, drive it everywhere. Of course we do. Who doesn't? And why wouldn't we? Once beliefs evolve to this level, it is very easy to add complementary beliefs without much difficulty.

From 1950 to 1970, the U.S. automobile population grew four times faster than the human population. Today, there are around 200 million cars in the United States.

POLITICS

As you can see, what we choose to believe is often determined by what messages we hear and images we are exposed to most often. As President George W. Bush once explained, "See, in my line of work, you've got to keep repeating things over and over and over again for the truth to sink in, to kind of catapult the propaganda." As a persuader, this statement should serve as a powerful reminder of the need for short compelling messages that you can send over and over again to underscore the importance of a point.

Here's an example of that propaganda catapult in action:

In a very self-revelatory 2003 *New York Times* article ("Keepers of Bush Image Lift Stagecraft to New Heights"), we got an inside glimpse at such a catapult as reporter Elisabeth Bumiller told us how the Bush administration was "using the powers of television and technology to promote a presidency like never before."

Bumiller reported, "The White House has stocked its communications operation with people from network television who have expertise in lighting, camera angles, and the importance of backdrops."

When President Bush spoke near Mount Rushmore in 2002, "the White House positioned the best platform for television crews off to one side, not head on as other White Houses have done, so that the cameras caught Mr. Bush in profile, his face perfectly aligned with the four presidents carved in stone."

"We pay particular attention to not only what the president says but what the American people see," Dan Bartlett, the White House communications director, unashamedly told Bumiller.

"Americans are leading busy lives, and sometimes they don't have the opportunity to read a story or listen to an entire broadcast," Bartlett added. "But if they can have an instant understanding of what the president is talking about by seeing sixty seconds of television, you accomplish your goals as communicators."

This goal of "instant understanding" for those Americans "leading busy lives" is a crucial component of persuasion that most persuaders miss. When confronted with an avalanche of information, people you are affecting will react most positively to messages that reach them at a core belief level, and is communicated in the shortest period of time. In other words, most people respond by running the message through a filter of "does this match my sense of reality and if so, I'll pay attention until I'm satiated." It is your responsibility as a persuader to build beliefs in your consumers that they will respond to. "Advertisements, getting a bargain, garage sales, and credit cards are firmly entrenched pillars of our way of life," says Harvard economist Juliet Schor. "We shop on our lunch hours, patronize outlet malls on vacation, and satisfy our latest desires with a late-night click of the mouse."

Managing persuasive compliance in our current society is all about setting standards and defining the accepted parameters.

CREATING NEW BELIEFS, ALTERING OLD ONES

Expertise

Psychologist Gregory Lester believes the task of challenging beliefs is "every bit as much philosophical and psychological as it is scientific and data-based." In other words, humans— whether viewed as citizens, consumers, or just people—respond to both emotional and logical stimulus. Evidence is crucial and convincing but often cannot trump the human need to fit in, and it is effective language and messaging that conveys both the logic and emotion in proper doses.

But there are several subliminally persuasive tactics to bear in mind. First, humans in general eagerly trust experts and voluntarily respect authority. Let's say you're sitting in a doctor's waiting room. Across the way, you watch a young mother with her energetic three-year-old son. Despite Mom's best efforts, the boy keeps trying to open the door leading to the outside corridor. Finally, the young mother tells him, "You better not go out there or the policeman in the hallway will arrest you." This little warning serves to keep the boy away from the door.

Of course, had the little boy worked up the nerve to open the door, he would've immediately discovered two facts:

1. There was no policeman in the hallway.
2. His mother sometimes lies to him.

From such relatively benign childhood experiences comes a familiarity, a comfort zone with trusting those in power: parents, teachers, police officers, members of the clergy, bosses, doctors, and so forth. Of course, this reality may be subject to exploitation, but it often is based in common sense. There are definitely occasions when deferring to a medical professional can be the prudent choice, for example, when your doctor presents the evidence to prove that cigarette smoking is detrimental to your health, you form a new belief—and in this case, one that can enhance your survival.

Perhaps the most notorious manifestation of obedience to authority is the Milgram Experiment. Stanley Milgram, a psychologist at Yale University, conducted a study in which "teachers" were asked to administer an electric shock to a "learner" for each mistake made during the experiment. (The teachers were not aware that the learners were hired actors and the electric shocks were fake.) As a result, 60 percent of the teachers obeyed orders and "punished" the learner with the highest possible voltage (450 volts), and 100 percent of the teachers willingly dished out at least 300 volts.

When ideas are presented from a position of authority, whether vested or created in the case of thought leaders, beliefs form more quickly. Many people will argue that our lack of critical thinking has caused many of the challenges facing our society today, and I wouldn't disagree. But, as a persuader, depending on your position, your goal is to gain compliance with an idea you are presenting, so the fastest way to gain compliance is to present yourself as an expert to the current beliefs. Make your argument congruent with the current belief set and you have a message that will be well received.

If you hope to change that belief, you start with a persuasive argument from a position of authority from experts. Those experts not only identify currently modifiable beliefs, they present with great authority the solution to the problem in the easiest possible way for people to understand it. Beliefs and values have much in common, and if you are to create beliefs that will endure, they need to support and evolve the values of the individual or group.

Ethical Expertise

In the words of pubic relations pioneer Edward Bernays, "Propaganda is of no use to the politician unless he has something to say which the public, consciously or unconsciously, wants to hear." The same sentiment might be applied to any authority figure or expert. Therefore, any form of marketing or publicity that utilizes an "expert" or a "voice of authority" in an honest manner will deftly play into this human condition without abusing it.

For a fine example of this technique that many see as being used for the greater good, let's return to the issue of global warming. None other than MTV has kicked off a campaign designed to educate its viewers about climate change. Offering information provided by, among others, the Natural Resources Defense

Council, the music network is relying on the time-proven tactic of citing "experts." While there remains some controversy about the causes or even the reality of global warming, it's difficult to imagine anything negative arising from MTV's efforts.

It's not unlike the mandatory seat belt law. While some of us fasten our seat belts to avoid getting a ticket, many more do so as a safety measure. We don't wait until we see another vehicle spinning out of control to snap the seat belt into place. We fasten it upon entering a car. It can be a little uncomfortable to wear, but if we arrive at our destination without needing that seat belt, we typically don't regret using it.

To apply this same mentality to climate change—to be unconcerned whether the human role in global warming is overstated—would be to live with a vision for the future. So, MTV and its partners are using public relations to create a new belief: why not alter our lifestyle as if our very existence were hanging in the balance?

Magic

The second secret mentioned earlier revolves around the fact that, at times, most humans very much *want* to be fooled. We *want* to believe in magic. Why else do we marvel at card tricks, sleight of hand, and other illusions? An existence in which every single act has been logically explained runs contrary to the typical human spirit and thus, many of us are ripe for the fooling.

As Exhibit A, consider the cautionary tale of marauding Martians landing in New Jersey.

On October 30, 1938—the night before Halloween—Orson Welles and his radio troupe, the Mercury Theater of the Air, put on a radio adaptation of the H. G. Wells science fiction novel, *The War of the Worlds.* Presented as if it were a newscast, the story of a deadly Martian invasion (beginning in the fictional Grover's Mill, New Jersey) was mistaken by many listeners to be true. Despite Welles's periodic interjections during the show that this was only a radio play, the result was mass hysteria. Americans, mostly in the Northeast, armed themselves, hit the road, hid in basements, and essentially panicked.

"All unwittingly, Mr. Orson Welles and the Mercury Theater of the Air have made one of the most fascinating and important demonstrations of all time," Dorothy Thompson later wrote in the *New York Tribune.* "They have proved that a few effective voices, accompanied by sound effects, can convince masses of people of a totally unreasonable, completely fantastic proposition as to create a nation-wide panic. They have demonstrated more potently than any argument, demonstrated beyond a question of a doubt, the appalling dangers and enormous effectiveness of popular and theatrical demagoguery."

Needless to say, there are lessons to learn from Welles's much-too-believable acting. Each of us retains a tiny bit of little kid in us and that little kid *wants* to be dazzled and maybe even deceived. We want to believe that wearing a particular article of clothing, eating a particular type of food, going to see a particular movie, or whatever, could result in an almost magical transformation and thus make us feel more confident or calm or sexy or successful or happy. (Remember what psychologist Gregory Lester said, "Beliefs are designed to operate independent of sensory data"). The trick, as it were—if you're seeking to meld ethics with profits—is to commence from a position of honesty.

Many of our best scholars see any attempt at persuasion as manipulation, discounting the idea that many people have legitimate needs and want to be educated. "What is the difference between unethical and ethical advertising?" asked anthropologist Vilhjalmur Stefansson. "Unethical advertising," he continued, "uses falsehoods to deceive the public; ethical advertising uses truth to deceive the public." This is a very dangerous view from the perspective of the persuader, but it is a good reminder that our job is not to deceive but to lead people to their own most logical conclusion, which happens to be the one you want them to have.

A BLACK BELT IN PERSUASION

Practitioners of certain martial arts—such as judo, aikido, and wing chun kung fu—understand and appreciate the principle of exploiting momentum. "The highest technique is to have no technique," Bruce Lee said. "My technique is a result of your technique; my movement is a result of your movement."

For example, a charging opponent can be met with a subtle redirection. Using "existing beliefs to persuade" can work in a similar manner.

We have learned that humans often create beliefs based on evidence. In other instances, the mere power of suggestion is enough. Sometimes, we are ready to believe in the fantastic—contrary to all common sense and logic. Regardless of the motivation, the creation of beliefs and the ensuing behavior these beliefs inspire are universal human qualities. This is the *momentum* mentioned earlier.

Those seeking to persuade customers to *believe* in their products or services are analogous to the martial arts master calmly surveying a situation. Recognizing that humans crave beliefs—*need* beliefs—the master welcomes this instinctual drive.

However, much like the aikido practitioners who guide an opponent into the direction of their choosing, those seeking to persuade must play on this natural human desire to embrace beliefs. If humans need to believe, why not aim that belief in *your* direction?

This requires innovation, endurance, and flexibility (much like martial arts training):

- *Innovation:* In a society based on information overload, originality always stands out, and uniqueness rarely goes unrecognized. It's logical to learn from those who came before you, but we must never be afraid to put our own stamp on our efforts.
- *Endurance:* "Modern propaganda," wrote Edward Bernays, "is a consistent, enduring effort to create or shape events to influence the relations of the public to an enterprise, idea or group." (See Chapter 2.) Remember: You're in this for the long haul.
- *Flexibility:* Sometimes you have to trust your instincts even if it means bending a few accepted norms. In the words of Bruce Lee: "All fixed set patterns are incapable of adaptability or pliability. The truth is outside of all fixed patterns."

HOW TO CREATE PERSUASIVE BELIEFS

From a very practical standpoint, I learned much about leveraging and creating new beliefs while growing up in a religious cult. I found that people were eager to move from one idea to the next when presented in context. They were very willing to modify their belief in ways sometimes not beneficial to themselves when the new belief supported an even deeper core belief like the idea of salvation or the difference between heaven and hell.

In most persuasion events, the choices that people make are not unlike the decisions around salvation; they are looking for a concept that is easy to understand and accept without having to think further.

To create beliefs in your audience:

- Build on existing beliefs and bridge those beliefs to the new idea.
- Create a highly charged environment where the lesson will be experienced with full emotional impact so that it is instantly imprinted as being real.
- Have authorities and experts present to deliver information crucial to acceptance of a new idea.
- Reduce the message to the smallest, hardest-hitting component possible and deliver it with great intensity.
- Repeat the message regularly and in multiple formats so that it becomes well accepted.
- Leverage social proof so that new believers become true believers. Allow them to quickly see that they are part of a group that sees things the same way.
- Reward their acceptance and adherence to the new belief through public and private recognition when possible. For example, you may offer them insider information (where legal) or make them part of an advisory group, and so on. The more authority people perceive that they have in a group, the more likely they are to spread the word of the group.

- Give the group both overt and covert ways of recognizing themselves when possible. A ribbon or a ring can be a powerful token that allows those in the know to recognize each other easily. Fraternal organizations like the Freemasons do this by wearing a ring that identifies their membership. Breast cancer research supporters wear a pink ribbon. People involved in religious practices often wear tokens of their affiliation like the Star of David or the crucifix. Covert means of recognition may include special phrases or words used to recognize each other. Alcoholics Anonymous did this effectively for many years by publicly calling their meetings gatherings of friends of Bill W.

Let me ask you a very important question right now: What beliefs do you hold about persuasion, sales, advertising, marketing, and public relations? Do those beliefs support you or keep you from being the most effective persuader you can be? Where did those beliefs develop? As you begin to understand your own beliefs and their roots, you'll better understand how to create powerful beliefs in your targeted audiences.

Implementation Is Everything
Money Follows Action

Before you read the next chapter, take the following actions:

Create messages that polarize people and that feed the desires of your supporters. The better the messages for your true believers (existing happy customers), the more likely they

---

are to become evangelists who will spread your message far and wide.

Develop your expert status. Be sure to have powerful opinions and share them.

Find the areas of your marketing, advertising, and sales process where you can deeply connect with the buyer's sense of identity. Play to their definition of who they are as a person or who they are as a company.

By deeply connecting with the existing beliefs of an audience, you are able to more quickly change their beliefs or enhance them. And people who accept other's beliefs as their own are much more likely to spread those beliefs and defend them. Belief making should be a core component of your marketing strategy.

ESSENTIAL FURTHER STUDY

Books

The 48 Laws of Power—Robert Greene (Viking, 1998)
Power vs. Force—David R. Hawkins (Hay House, 1995)
Battle for the Mind—William Sargant (Malor Books, 1997)

Viral Video and Web Sites

Mutant Milk: youtube.com/watch?v=h0awf4sinso&feature= related

Movies

Our Brand Is Crisis—Koch Lorber Films (2005)
Marjoe—New Video Group (1972)
Jesus Camp—Magnolia (2006)

7

HARNESS THE POWER OF THE PEOPLE'S MEDIA

Our Age of Anxiety is, in great part, the result of trying to do today's jobs with yesterday's tools.

The new media are not bridges between man and nature; they are nature.

— Marshall McLuhan

The fear of loss of control of the traditional mass media by the corporations that run them has less to do with the media than it does with their ability to control ideas. That control of ideas is where the profit is, not the medium through which the ideas are disseminated.

Traditional media have long been able to choose what and whose ideas best suited a public that looked to them as a source of all things new and interesting. The People's Media, which includes blogs, online video, social networking sites, self-publishing, podcasting, and teleseminars, took away their death grip on the mind of the public at large and opened the doors for anyone to be a mass influencer. The balance of power is shifting, and as it does, the traditionalists scramble to find a way to regain control. They cling to what is left of their influence like a beggar clutches his rags against the winter's chill. Adaptation and emulation is their only chance for survival as the People's Media evolve at a superhuman pace.

THE POWER OF THE PEOPLE'S MEDIA

When average people discovered that they had the ability to share their ideas widely with just a few strokes of a keyboard and the click of a mouse, the balance of power began to change.

Before easy access to media, the consolidation of ideas and messages took much longer than it now requires. People had to spend a great deal of time focused on patiently spreading their message through whatever media they could get into; fads built over time. Today, fads can come and go in just a couple of months. Ideas are generated, shared, acted on, and abandoned in the amount of time it takes to mount a strong public relations campaign.

The People's Media are highly believable because no matter what your interest, you'll find large groups of people just like you eager to connect and share information. Once those people connect, they are a viable force that can influence large numbers of people quickly when they leverage their personal networks.

The People's Media are also believable because the information is coming from sources other than the sources which have long since lost much of their credibility: the government, corporations, academia. Now, individuals who might have otherwise faced censorship are able to share infectious ideas, good or bad. If they understand the lessons of influence learned in traditional media, they can spread those messages rapidly, and develop a following of willing adherents.

INFLUENCE LESSONS FROM TRADITIONAL MEDIA

1. Information presented by a trusted source is accepted with little critical thinking: Traditional media spend large sums of money to create trusted newscasters, writers, and show hosts with whom you develop a relationship and trust. Once the relationship has developed, the consumer will accept whatever ideas are presented as being correct, even if she disagrees with the idea. As long as the host, newscaster, or reporter doesn't present the information as his own, if he presents it as an observer, the relationship continues safely and comfortably. If he occasionally challenges obviously bad ideas or lies, he gains even more trust and credibility.

   • The lesson for the subliminal persuader is to develop a following of people who look to you for their information and interpretation of events. Report and interpret ideas in ways that are congruent with the beliefs of your audience. Challenge the status quo, or if appropriate, support it, but build more interesting interpretations or allow access to people your audience wouldn't normally have access to. Slowly introduce new ideas once you've gained trust, and the ideas will be accepted.

2. Frequency is the key to creating long-term beliefs: The more people hear something from sources they trust, the faster they believe it. And, the more they hear it, the faster they spread it.

   - Frequency is a powerful subliminal persuader because people don't equate hearing something multiple times from multiple sources as an attempt to persuade; they simply see it as mounting evidence that something is true. It creates an internal sense of urgency and acceptance.

3. Sensationalism sells: The more controversial something is, the more it exposes something, the more it creates drama, the more people listen, watch, and read. There is a reason that people like Paris Hilton or Britney Spears "accidentally" expose themselves in public. It creates drama that the media need to get you interested. All good stories need an antagonist, drama, conflict, and resolution for it to be interesting. The more you lead with the raw sensational hook, the more likely you are to create awareness and to get people to talk about what you did.

   - Sensationalism persuades because it works on the most base of our emotions. It focuses on shock, surprise, anger, revulsion, or intense curiosity. Ask yourself where can you be a reporter in a firestorm? Can you enter the maelstrom and report on it for those who want to sit in the comfort of their home and read about it or watch your guerrilla video on YouTube? Sometimes the sensationalism only serves the purpose of connecting the people to you rather than creating your own drama that people can respond to. A current example of this kind of sensationalism, which has raised awareness and ire and won great praise from the public (and a growing outrage by the legal community), is NBC's TV show "To Catch A Predator." The show focuses on catching child sexual predators in the act. But the real positive recipient of the attention is the web site pervertedjustice.com.

4. Conversation domination: Howie Schwartz was the first person I heard use this term in relationship to the People's Media, but it applies to traditional media as well. If you want to dominate a conversation and be the de facto leader, you create the conversation and you may even have the conversation with others whom you encourage or even develop into experts on the topic.

   • When you dominate a conversation by creating the conversation in the first place, it is very easy to move ideas forward. The ideas are created by you and those you endorse or create, present your ideas and opinions as their own to create awareness. They are highly persuasive because the only place that people can learn about the conversation is from you or those you endorse. A commonly used tactic online is the use of an avatar. In Hindu mythology, an avatar is the descent of a deity to the earth in an incarnate form or some manifest shape, that is, the incarnation of a god. In online usage, an avatar is an assumed identity used to identify oneself or persona online. Avatars are widely used in online persuasion and often unethically in online manipulation. Used correctly, they are no more insidious than a pen name or a stage name.

> **Subliminal Sales Secret**
>
> If you want to persuade better in person or in your advertising, leverage the key principles of media persuasion. Create a persona, an expert who is the voice of the industry, the voice of reason, the voice of the future in your industry. Ensure that the voice is heard on a regular basis in multiple media to better spread the ideas that lead to support and purchase of your products, services, or ideas. Create controversy to speed up the awareness and the conversation. Controversy can come in many forms beyond outright argument. Controversy can be introducing ideas that are counter to currently held beliefs, expansive future views, revelations of weaknesses in the industry or best-of-class products (this can be done effectively by using an avatar).
>
> By using these very powerful, time-tested techniques in person and in your advertising you'll quickly be able to own significant mindshare in your target audience.

A word of caution is in order here. Reputation management is a key element you need to concern yourself with when you use the traditional media influence tactics. You must be ethical and not create fire where none exists. If you expose yourself as a fraud, you'll be remembered for that faster and longer than any goodwill you create through careful and appropriate application of the principles.

> Allow me to give you an example. Ben Mack and I were demonstrating this principle on Michel Fortin's Copywriters Board (copywritersboard.com). Rather than tell people first that we

were going to demonstrate the principle, we simply did it. Ben and I staged an argument on the board that got very heated and personal. Our goal was that someone who knew both of us would call us out on it and we'd reveal the technique. The process was very effective, it got hundreds of views in just a few days and many comments. But, we made two critical mistakes. First, we didn't tell the board leadership what we were doing; we wrongly assumed they'd understand. Second, we let it go too long without revealing the lesson. The result was that some people were offended. The value of the lesson was lost in the execution of the tactic because it was not fully thought out. Some people felt fooled by the whole thing and that made them very vocal in a not so positive way about us. In the end, everyone understood the lesson and the lesson that we learned and hopefully our reputations as helpers in the group overcame the angst. But, to some people, we'll always be the guys who played a dirty joke in a special group of people and they'll revile us for it.

Reputation management is a key to subliminal persuasion in the People's Media.

WHICH MEDIUM AND HOW?

When it comes to the People's Media, the choices advance every day, and certainly by the time you read this, it may have evolved new media not discussed here. That said, the key media that you can leverage today and for quite some time to come are:

Blogs
Online video

Social networks

Teleseminars

Podcasting

Self-publishing

Blogs

Blogs have become ubiquitous online and are one of the most potent tools for the subliminal persuader. The ease with which a blog can be created and populated with information makes them a first choice for creating influence using the People's Media. This is not a book on the technicalities of setting up a blog, but if you can type using Microsoft Word, you can set up a blog through wordpress.org (a free, open source web site) or typepad.com (a subscription-supported web site).

Search engines love blogs because of the recency and relevancy to searches. You'll often find that well-crafted blog posts will regularly show up in the top 10 organic search positions.

When people search online, they have a sense that they are in control of the information that they consume, and as a result, tend to believe more of what they find that resonates with them. What most don't realize is that mass influencers are very focused on understanding how searches occur so they can be sure that their messages show up where their potential audience searches.

There are several criteria for making blogs effective persuasion tools.

The first criterion is that the blog must be relevant to the target audience and the information must be current. There is a temptation to cover too much ground or too many varied issues in one blog to fill space. This is *always* the wrong idea if you are trying to create a highly persuasive environment. The deeper into the topic you take someone, the more they become connected to you. There are two blogs that are phenomenal at leveraging this idea, sethgodin.typepad.com and micropersuasion.com. Study both of them to see how to become highly influential without seeming obvious. Of course, you'll want to study the blog associated with this book for even more detailed strategies and interviews with top subliminal influencers.

The second key to an effective blog is to take people places they may not have discovered on their own. Show them places, thoughts, and ideas they will find intriguing . . . and then create influence by helping them interpret what they are seeing and experiencing. Offer explanations of the information they are consuming. Direct them to other supportive sites so they can build some intensity around your ideas and begin to make them their own.

The third criterion is to direct them to actions. Start with small steps by getting them to disclose personal information. For example, have them give you their name and e-mail address in exchange for some privileged information or to be able to participate in an inner circle.

Finally, make them part of the conversation by allowing them to comment and share their ideas so they can become fervent supporters. Offer them insights into the effectiveness of spreading their ideas and messages. Publicly acknowledge their ideas and contributions. This is where readers become converts and converts become evangelists. And evangelists bring people hungry for your brand of salvation . . . more on that in a few chapters when I talk about building a cult following.

Subliminal Selling Secret

When you create your blog posts, be sure that you use your high value key words and search terms, along with any conversation domination-created term in your post headline. Also, be sure to repeat them a few times throughout the post body to increase the relevance of the post. Finally, be sure that you tag your post with the same terms to make it easy for searchers to find you.

To increase the awareness of the post and the value to the search engines, get your readers to go to Digg.com and Digg your story, or to stumbleupon.com and stumble it. High Digg and Stumpleupon rankings make the story more valuable and likely to be found online. The same is true at Technorati.com. Have people become fans of your blog at Technorati. Condition your readers to Digg every post, and make it easy for them by putting the Digg widget on your blog. If that last sentence made no sense to you at all, don't worry, just say it to the person who sets up your blog, and like magic, they'll make it appear.

Online Video

Google Video and YouTube have made distribution of video as simple as uploading a file, and it's free. That means virtually anyone can create powerfully persuasive video productions and begin influencing immediately. Before online video, citizen-created video was relegated to the realm of public access cable television, which is rarely viewed. On the other hand, there are literally millions of searches a day on Google Video and YouTube.

Video allows you to connect with your growing audience in a whole new way. They actually get to see you and hear you.

They get to use all of their senses to evaluate you. To effectively use video, keep them under five minutes. Make a single point and drive it home with frequency.

You can create television quality video using the free video editing software that comes with both a PC and the Macintosh and a simple handheld camera. The camera I recommend is the Canon Powershot SD series (the current model as of this writing is the SD1000). You can carry this tool with you everywhere you go. The camera itself is smaller than a deck of cards and shoots up to 60 frames per second of video. You can create a video wherever you are as long as you have enough light. And, demonstrating what you are talking about or reporting on others doing it makes you a reporter and a valuable source of information.

Focus on interpreting what the viewers are seeing to make your videos subliminally persuasive. Use the visual element to show them proof of what you are saying. Nothing persuades like firsthand experience. You can capture events, interviews with interesting people, and demonstrations of how to do something specific using your product or idea as the prominent tool.

When you create video, focus on your persona; remember that you are persuading subliminally. Be sure that you are congruent with the message you are sharing. Be sure you are appropriately dressed to influence your audience. Focus on your voice, make it smooth, engaging, and varied so that you are interesting to listen to. Take control if you are interviewing people, be direct in your questions, and dig in to get the answers your audience needs to see and hear.

Like all media, the key to success with video is content and relevancy. If you give people interesting content that they can consume, and you tie it in with blog posts where they have a chance to scan information and dip deeper with video, you have created a highly compelling format that you can use to deeply influence your audience.

Social Networks

Social networks like Facebook.com, Myspace.com, Twitter .com, and Linkedin.com have become massive gathering places for like-minded people. Let me give you an example. Go to Facebook.com right now and search for my name. If you don't have an account, set one up while you are there so you can see the power of this medium. Notice the number of friends I have and pick any one of them and see the number he has. You see how quickly you can connect with about anyone you want. It adds a whole new twist to the idea of six degrees of separation. Now that you've found me, click on the link for groups and in the search box type in *persuasion* and *influence.* There you'll find a whole host of like-minded people who are eager to discuss persuasion, influence, and marketing and who are eager to share their ideas and insights. Sign up and be a part to see how blindingly effective this medium can be.

This medium is effective because it is the ultimate referral system. People who are your friends are very likely to be receptive to your ideas and to helping you.

You can also create forums, groups, and blogs inside many of these social networking sites, and they're all free. Searching out people with like-minded interests is very easy, and allows you to quickly build a sphere of influence among people who are already actively communicating among themselves.

Teleseminars

Teleseminars are a logical extension of videos and blogs. These are interactive live events by phone where you can more deeply influence an audience that wants to hear from you. Think of teleseminars as syndication for the average person.

The goal with teleseminars is to provide timely, hot topic information to your most interested followers. Again, like most of the People's Media, this is a nearly free medium for you. You can get a free bridge line that will allow you to speak to up to 1,000 people simultaneously at freeconferencecall.com or highspeedconferencing.com.

Once you've set up your free account, you need only let people know the date and time that you'll be conducting your teleseminar, and you can educate everyone who calls in. You also have the option of having a two-way conversation, you can take questions, debate, or do anything else you want that furthers your point. This is again highly subliminally effective because of the deep level of engagement the phone has. People are conditioned to interacting with the phone in a very specific way and they fall into this subconscious routine the moment they pick up the phone. They also often enter a light trance state on the phone, making persuasion even more effective.

Coaching by phone or in person is another powerful persuasion tool that you can leverage, and I've included a special guide on persuasive coaching by Dr. Rachna Jain, the Coach Creator, in the appendix. Dr. Jain is a psychologist who will explain why coaching is highly persuasive and how you can leverage it. For a great example of persuasive coaching in action, visit masterpersuasionnow.com.

Group persuasion by phone is one of the most effective tools you can develop. It is the next best thing to being live in front of a group for gaining mass compliance. When I do teleseminars, I typically gain persuasive compliance (measured by the actions they take) of 20 to 50 percent of the attending audience.

Podcasting

Podcasting is the creation of audio programs that are available for automated downloads to mp3 players. The idea has great potential, but in reality, has not yet achieved the level of consumer acceptance that the industry thought it would.

But that isn't really important. It is effective when used appropriately.

Like video, podcasts should be very short and designed to communicate an idea quickly and completely. One of the ways I like to use podcasts is to reinforce ideas that I'm promoting in all of the other media. I'll create a brief podcast, for example, on the topic of using subliminal persuasion, to upsell at the retailer's cash register. I'll upload it to iTunes and libsyn.com so that people can download it. I'll make people aware of it in my blog, but I'll do something else and this is what makes it more effective as a persuasion tool. First, link directly to audio in your blog posts and build a post that supports what you are explaining. Second, use it to support your selling efforts on your web site by putting a play button next to a product or service so that people can listen to you as you explain why they should use the product or service.

Audio (like radio) is an effective persuasion medium, and to the extent that you can get people to actually download or listen to the audio, you can have a great impact.

Audio is also very effective when you use coaching as a tool to persuade.

Self-Publishing

Being an author offers you tremendous credibility in your targeted audience. Also, being an author is easier than it ever has been, thanks to self-publishing.

When you create a nonfiction book giving instruction on a topic that the audience desires, you get to influence their thinking for as many pages as you choose. The book allows you to lay out the decision criteria they should use, the buying criteria they should use, and allows you to build arguments that they can buy into over time.

In my first persuasion book, *Persuasion: The Art of Getting What You Want*, I laid out a complete process for writing a book quickly.

If I had to reinvent myself tomorrow and build a following fast, the first thing I'd do is write a book. A book is also highly effective in opening doors, getting past gatekeepers, and generating income fast.

But the real reason that books are so effective as subliminal persuasion tools is that they instantly identify you as an expert. People naturally choose experts over others when given a choice. There is less risk in choosing an expert. Books also indicate a certain level of intellectual mastery beyond the topic at hand, which also makes people comfortable. Most people feel like they could never write a whole book on a topic and feel that people who can have already done something they can't, so it isn't a big stretch to accept the proposal that the author is presenting them with.

The overarching persuasion strategy with the People's Media is to create a confluence of information focused on you and your ideas. The more that people hear about you, the more influential you become to them. By creating your own media empire, you create a following that is dedicated and highly compliant.

Implementation Is Everything

Money Follows Action

Before you read the next chapter, take the following actions:

- Write out a one-page or back-of-napkin plan about how you'll begin leveraging the People's Media.
- Sign up for Facebook at facebook.com and invite me to be your friend so that you can start instantly expanding your online network. Also, search the facebook.com groups for Persuasion and Influence and join the group.
- Visit masterpersuasionnow.com.

ESSENTIAL FURTHER STUDY

Books

Secrets of Online Persuasion—John Paul and Deborah Micek (Morgan James, 2006)

On Writing Well—William Zinsser (HarperCollins, 2006)

Authority Site Black Book—Available for free download at authorityblackbook.com

Movies

McLuhan's Wake (National Film Board of Canada, 2003)

8

DELIVER THE
EXPERIENCE

*I have but one lamp by which my feet are guided, and that
is the lamp of experience. I know no way of judging of the
future but by the past.*

— British historian Edward Gibbon

Persuasion, sales, marketing, and influence all make overt and
implied promises to the person being persuaded. Subliminal
persuaders make the most imperceptible promises. But those
subliminal promises create an expectation of something the
audience believes will occur.

Your audience will also judge you by the experiences they've
had in the past or the predominant experience that the industry
has conditioned them to believe is correct. But, when you understand the influential power of experience, you'll understand how
you can create the experience against which every other experience is judged. And that is one of the most profitable places

you can be. The reason this is so popular goes back to Gibbon's quote; your customers will always use the lamp of experience to judge the future. If you can give them the lamp that illuminates the future in your favor, you'll own them for life.

When a magician appears to drop a coin from one hand to another but palms it instead, the mind sees the coin as having fallen into the second hand. This is called sight retention and allows the expectant viewers to have a magical experience. When the mind follows the coin and the coin doesn't appear, the illusion is complete and the viewer experiences exactly what was expected.

In persuasion, the promises we make and the expectations that we set are the beliefs that those we persuade hope will occur. When they don't, magic doesn't happen. In fact, just the opposite happens, an unpleasant confrontation occurs that breaks the spell of persuasion and can doom the relationship.

Experience is the subtlest of persuaders; it is a tangible expectation that, when met, creates deep reinforcement of the influence strategies you've implemented so far.

Most persuasion training stops at compliance, which is a mistake. Compliance occurs when they agree to engage with you, but real compliance doesn't occur until after they complete the expected course of action and enjoy the expected experience.

EXPECTATIONS

For persuasion to be most effective you have to set expectations early and often. Expectation is anticipation of an experience that is to occur in the future.

The more overt the expectation, the more specific the experience must be for congruence. The more general or subtle the expectation, the more room you have in creating an experience. It is imperative when you are developing your persuasion strategies that you compare the current experience your audience has to the expectation, and create an experience that matches or exceeds that expectation.

MASS EXPECTATIONS

Consumers today have come to expect an experience that is part theater, part magic, and always exceptional. There are too many examples of great experiences that people can point to as the model they expect. Some of the experiences that people consider exceptional today happen at:

Disneyland
The Cheesecake Factory
Starbucks
The W Hotel
FAO Schwarz
American Girl
Hard Rock Café
Jimmy Buffett's Margaritaville (or concert)

With expectations of amazing experiences being set higher every day, it is imperative that you create an experience you can control and guarantee to exceed the expectations of your audience. If you don't, they'll revert to previous or imagined expectations of the experience.

FANTASY

You need to understand that to deeply persuade through an experience, you are inviting someone into a fantasy world. That fantasy world is one in which he is the hero and is able to create whatever he wants.

Marjoe Gortner was the nation's youngest Pentecostal minister. He performed his first wedding ceremony when he was four years old. You might ask how a four-year-old would know how to marry someone, much less actually do it. Well, he had a lot of help from his mother, who taught him exactly how to act and what to do. She also asphyxiated him to help him remember his Scripture.

Marjoe had a number of personal revelations as he grew older. One was that he was no longer a believer and that he didn't want to keep manipulating people. He also had a revelation about the people. He discovered that for people who were not allowed to watch television, dance, or participate in most forms of entertainment, the tent meetings he performed in were their entertainment, and he was the entertainer. To that extent, he treated each sermon like a rock concert and emulated Mick Jagger. If you search for Marjoe on YouTube you'll find several examples of him preaching, and if you watch his movements, you'll see Mick Jagger.

Marjoe understood the fantasy that people were experiencing when he performed and he met them where they were. By speaking to people where they are, you can move them to where you want them to go, but you have to meet them where they are first.

When you set out to persuade the masses, you must understand their fantasy. Once you understand what the special experience they want to have is, you can easily create it. If they don't understand what their fantasy world looks like, they are even more susceptible to persuasion at that point, because they will allow you to create the fantasy for them. If you get to create the fantasy, yours will always be the experience they compare to.

Televangelists understand this entry into fantasy better than most.

ENTERING THE FANTASY

Influence occurs when you enter the fantasy and meet the expectations. When a person experiences their fantasy coming true, they are ecstatic. It is that feeling of ecstasy that remains when the experience ends, that drives them back, that causes them to tell their friends about it, to proselytize to their network, and to encourage them to experience what they did.

Here's how a televangelist enters the fantasy. He looks into the camera and speaks with emotional intensity and sincerity. "God is telling me that there is a little old woman out there watching right now who has twenty dollars hidden away in her cookie jar and He wants you to get that money and send it in to Jesus right now." Knowing his audience, he understands that there are dozens, if not hundreds, of "little old women" watching who feel that they are being spoken to directly and who send in their cash.

I don't want people to think I'm taking a stab at religion here; I'm not. And, televangelists are not the only ones who are exceptional at entering the fantasy and intensifying the experience. The purveyors of real estate courses, direct marketing courses, and other get-rich-quick programs on late night television do it equally well. The good-looking (or average-looking) guy is being interviewed by one or more beautiful women with large breasts and revealing clothes. He is being interviewed in a tropical location or inside a beautiful home. He reveals how not long ago he was working long hours in a dead-end job and he saw an offer just like this one and he decided to try it out and his life was changed. Look around him, he lives a life of opulence and the beautiful women fawn over his wealth and prowess. The fantasy is complete. Buying the package will lead to wealth and wealth leads to gorgeous women who want to have sex with self-made men.

You had one of two fantasies when you bought this book. One was that there are secrets that "they" don't want you to know about influence and marketing. But you want to know the secrets, because if you do, you'll become even more effective at getting the things that you want. This, by the way, is true, and so is the fact that by necessity as you learn the skills, the fantasy changes. You may even become jaded by what become very obvious attempts to enter your reality and persuade you. The second fantasy is that you are hyperaware of the attempts of media and corporations to manipulate your experience, and that the best defense is knowledge. For you, this book is nearly sacred, because it reveals exactly how persuasion, influence, coercion, and manipulation occur. It is the shield you can wield to protect yourself and your loved ones from the perils of persuasion.

A lot of people (mostly other persuasion experts) were concerned that I'd be making a mistake by revealing the two fantasies that sell this book . . . but I have my own fantasy that involves understanding how intelligent you are and how you'll use these techniques for the betterment of the world around us. In my fantasy, persuasion is used to solve some of the most important issues facing the world today and to make profits more easily and predictably.

A company that did a phenomenal job of entering my fantasy and creating an experience that I couldn't resist is an organization called guideon.org. Guideon.org does two very important things. They provide mentorship and education for children of military members who lost their lives in the war in Iraq or Afghanistan. They provide the children and their surviving parents a camp where they can be together with other people like them, to learn new skills for coping and adjusting. They provide them with an experience of a lifetime to help to some degree counter the worst experience of a young life. The second thing they do is provide final wishes. They find out what the parent who was killed promised to do with their kids when they got back and they make those last wishes happen.

Just as effectively as the televangelist who reaches out to the "little old woman," they reached out to me, the "veteran who wants to make a difference for American children affected by the war." In my fantasy, I could imagine nothing more important than helping children learn how to appropriately navigate their grief and to get complete. So I immediately set to work. I introduced them to Russell Friedman of the Grief Recovery Institute (grief.net) and co-author of *When Children Grieve.* The Grief Recovery Institute is the nation's foremost resource for grievers and those who work with them. I also started telling everyone I know about the amazing work that this organization is doing. And, I included it in my book, where tens of thousands of people will learn about them. Many of you will feel as compelled as I did to make a donation to help a grieving child.

And why was I so compelled? Because I could literally feel the pain of losing a parent. I lost my own mother when I was young to a cult, and she died when I was still young. I completely experienced the pain they were trying to help heal, and as a result I was compelled. For me, that felt a lot like a lump in my throat that led me to make a donation. What does your experience feel like?

This idea of fantasy is so important that I want to leave you with one last example. My wife owns very successful wellness spas called Breathe Wellness Spas. When she created the spas, she was very clear about the fantasy that the people who would be coming had. They expected physical healing in the lap of luxury. They wanted to feel better physically and emotionally by coming to one place and spending money once. So the experience begins the moment they call. They are greeted warmly; time isn't an issue on the phone. When they arrive, they are offered small luxuries like chocolates, fruit, or wine. They are greeted by name. Everyone from the greeter to the therapist is focused on delivering the experience. They are treated with the utmost respect. They are surprised at every step of the way. They are given unexpected treatment that heightens the experience of extreme pampering and relaxation. They are offered the opportunity to talk or just sink into bliss. Therapists literally tell each client that they won't speak to them after the initial consultation unless the client chooses to speak; that they should focus on the depth of their relaxation. When their service is complete, they are given water or juice again . . . in fine crystal goblets or very high-end wine glasses. The result is that people find themselves in a sanctuary that they don't want to leave and that they want to get back to as soon as they can, preferably with friends. Their fantasy is that they want to escape, to be treated as royalty, to be relieved of their stress and be heard if they so choose, or to be one with themselves. It is also a very natural extension of the experience to take home products that allow them to try to recreate that sanctuary at home. They'll never ultimately be as successful on their own, so they'll always return. Delivering this kind of experience was so powerful, that when my wife and I moved to Virginia, her core clients were so unhappy with the alternative experiences, that they literally got together and got her to come back to Boise regularly to massage them. They were willing to pay a great deal more to have the experience that fulfilled the fantasy.

Fantasy is where people live and experience the reality that they want. Carefully evaluate your customer's fantasy and see where you can enter it. Once you understand the fantasy, you can intensify the experience. And when you intensify the experience, persuasion happens.

ATMOSPHERICS

In 1973, marketing professor Phillip Kotler introduced the world to the science of atmospherics in the *Journal of Retailing*. According to Kotler, *atmospherics* is "The conscious planning of atmospheres to contribute to the buyer's purchasing propensity."

You've likely heard me say that businesses have a persona. Atmospherics are the persona of your business. Creating a business persona is consciously creating an atmosphere that increases the buyer's purchasing propensity. Every bit of the experience is orchestrated from the way your web site looks, to the way your building looks, to the way your staff looks and is trained to engage the buyer to the way your product is designed or your service is delivered. The extent to which you can deliver an emotionally charged experience that fits the fantasy the buyer expects, will determine how profitable you'll ultimately be and the long-term effectiveness of your persuasion strategies.

I want you to ask yourself the following questions to determine what the atmosphere (and experience) is that you are delivering.

- What is the fantasy that my client has, and how do I acknowledge and reinforce it from the first point of contact?
- What is the experience people have when they call me?
- What is the experience that people have when they get to my web site?
- What are the implicit and explicit promises that I'm making to my audience?
- What can I do to intensify the fantasy and increase the experience?
- Am I setting criteria for the experience where one doesn't exist so that I can control the experience in the future?
- Do my building, my furnishings, or my staff create an emotionally compelling experience for people who come to my office or store?
- What are the three most important things I could do or change to intensify the emotional experience of the people who engage me?
- What is one thing that I can do that leaves an indelible experience in the buyer who engages me so that I own a dominant position of influence in his mind in the future?

Subliminal Selling Secret

Sometimes, when working to create an experience, people get stuck because they can't seem to figure out what people really want from the experience. One of the best ways to find out is to ask ... but in a very specific way.

I like to ask people about the "good old days," so I'll ask them to recount their first experience in the category. Their first experience may have been amazing or it may have been bad. Either way, it gives you a basis for determining where they are now.

Once they explain their first experience, I start asking them feeling questions, questions like, "How did you feel about _____?" Or, "When you think about _____, how does that make you feel?" Another great question is, "What will it be like when you find the perfect solution?" Or, "If you could wave a magic wand and create the perfect buying experience around this, what would that be like?"

By simply asking these kinds of questions, you can gather a great deal of emotional information that you can leverage in building your experience. Listen closely as people relate their experiences. They'll give you reams of emotional content that you can feed back to them as measured by the experience they will have with you.

In a coming chapter, I discuss how to create a cult of customers. A lot of people banter that word around as if they know what it means. Most don't and most cults of customers arise organically. But the most profitable ones are carefully cultivated. Cults form around experiences, as you'll discover.

MAKE THE BUYER THE HERO

No matter whether your intention is to persuade the masses or the individual, you have to remember that you are really only persuading one person at a time. The conversation you have, or the experience you create, has to feel like it is unique to the person experiencing it. She needs to feel that it is directed at her personally because she must feel like she is in control of her decision for persuasion to occur. All persuasion is self-persuasion from the perspective of the individual who is complying with your efforts to get her to take a particular course of action.

Once you understand the fantasy that your audience has, and you know what experience you must deliver, you have to decide how to make the individual the hero. Everyone you persuade is looking for the emotional contentment that feeling like a hero brings. They want to feel like they did something good and powerful for themselves, their family, their company, or the world around them. They want to not only be recognized, but they must recognize that they are truly heroic for what they've done.

Heroics sounds very strong, but we need to put it in context. We are not talking about walking into a burning building or charging a machine gun emplacement.

Heroics in the eyes of the person being persuaded is simply the emotional contentment that comes from making a considered decision that feels right. You help people feel heroic when you help them experience an enhancement in the quality of their life in some way. The more they feel unique, or better, on the inside, or smarter than those around them, the more heroic their decision feels.

Many people confuse heroics with being gutsy, and that is a part of the hero fantasy that you can leverage. When

you get people to take public actions first, you talk about
their intelligence, their courage, and their willingness to do
something that others have difficulty doing. They find clarity
in what others perceive as confusion, and they take action.
For most people, that feels very heroic. In what ways can you
engage people in experiencing those things with you?

Something I do in many of the talks I do where I sell something from the stage is to get people to come to the front in the
very beginning of the talk and give me their money or credit
card. When they do and nothing happens, they don't lose their
money, and they aren't tricked into anything. There is actually
a lesson there. They feel very good about having the courage
to get up to the front of the room and participate. They begin
having an experience.

Subliminal Selling Secret

When you create a hero, someone who has gone first, taken
an action that is perceived to be dangerous or uncertain, you
expose them to the world. Heroes feel most like heroes when
they are exposed as such. People who feel like they've taken
heroic action are also much more likely to become evangelists
for your product, because telling their story of success makes
them feel heroic all over again. One of the core desires that
drive persuasion is the desire of people to feel special.

I want you to start thinking of persuasion as theater and
those that you'll persuade as an audience. Once you begin to
realize that everything you are doing is related to creating a
memorable experience, your business will change. Your position as a persuader will change.

When you think of your job not as a persuader but as an actor, you begin to think differently about delivering an experience. Now, please understand I'm not giving you license to lie or engage your customers in fiction. I'm giving you license to carefully orchestrate and deliver a magical experience that can't be forgotten or easily replaced by a competitor.

Your office is your stage. The furnishings are your staging, the décor the scenery. They must be carefully placed and designed to create the atmosphere that the audience expects so they can engage themselves in your story. Your employees are your players. Each of them must be carefully choreographed to play his part. They must emotionally engage with the buyer to move the scene forward to conclusion. When everything is in place and everyone plays his part to perfection, the audience is moved, and compelled. They experience the magic they always knew existed.

You never forget your first kiss, your first love, your first pure adrenaline-filled adventure . . . and you never forget the first time a person or a company delivered an experience that was unbelievable. Everything that comes after is a comparison that mostly doesn't live up to the first experience.

Implementation Is Everything

Money Follows Action

Before you read the next chapter, take the following actions:

- Question at least three of your best clients or customers about their experience with you. Find out if there is something you could add that would make their experience

---

exceptional. Write down the emotional components of their discussion and evaluate the experience against those emotions. See if you need to do more and where you can enter their fantasy most effectively.

- Visit at least two or three experience-oriented or themed businesses and take notes about how they create the specific experience. Look at their décor, their attitude, and their employees. Notice how they create the theater and how it relates to the experience you expect and the experience you have. Notice how it feels when you are treated in a well-choreographed way. See where the choreography leads you as measured by opportunities to buy.

- Visit guideon.org and experience how an organization that is making a difference at an individual level creates an experience for you. If you like what they are doing, give them a donation. You'll be a part of something much bigger than any of us and you'll make an unbelievable difference for some very special kids. And, if you love what they are doing, send a note to a few of your friends and influence them to do the same.

ESSENTIAL FURTHER STUDY

Books

- *The Experience Economy*—B. Joseph Pine II and James ~~Read~~ H̶ H. Gilmore (Harvard Business School Press, 1999)
  Coercion—Douglas Rushkoff (Riverhead Books, 2000)
  Why People Buy Things They Don't Need—Pamela Danziger (Dearborn, 2003)

Movies

Search YouTube for Marjoe Gortner and visit subliminal persuasionbook.com for some unexpected resources.

Television

Choose at least two televangelists and two infomercials to watch to see how they deliver on the fantasy. I suggest that one televangelist you watch be Joel Osteen, and pick at least one real estate investment infomercial.

9

THE SUBLIMINAL POWER OF WORDS

Handle them carefully, for words have more power than atom bombs.

— Author and poet Pearl Strachan Hurd

While it seems so obvious that words have great power to persuade, in fact, I'd argue that words are the basis for all persuasion. Your words either persuade you or you use your words to persuade another person.

The simplest of words lathered on the heart of stone can cause the hard exterior to reveal the beating cradle of human connectedness. The same words hurled like spears can pierce the soul, leaving behind an empty vessel to wander the earth with a wound that can be healed only by better words not often found.

As a persuader, it is important that you completely understand the great responsibility that comes with learning how to use words. Words can be weapons of mass destruction (deception), and as levers and fulcrums for change, and all have their place. It is up to you to choose how you'll use your words.

The subliminal power of words comes with your ability to speak to different parts of the person you are influencing. You may move him to emotion, to action, to inaction, or to intense rage to create change. But it won't be you or the words themselves, it will be the combinations you choose and the intensity with which they are delivered.

Roy Williams, the author of *The Wizard of Ads* and founder of Wizard Academy (wizardacademy.com) does some of the most fascinating exposition on words that I've ever seen. Thanks, Roy! In one exercise, he starts out by getting people pumped on Bruce Springsteen's rock anthem "Born in the U.S.A."

"Born in the U.S.A." is an anthem whose music gets the blood pumping of most everyone who hears it and fills hearts with pride. When you take a close look at the words, however, cleverly disguised by amazing music, the feeling begins to change. The lyrics actually tell the story of a beaten-down veteran who was abandoned by the United States and the system he fought for. If you've never read the actual lyrics of "Born in the U.S.A.," I strongly suggest that you google them and read them now. Words, when combined with something that distract, can paint a completely different picture and engage us deeply subliminally. They even often confuse us to the extent that we praise the U.S.A. for abandoning one of its own after he served his country in the name of patriotism.

ATTENTION

The first key in subliminal language is being heard. You must have a powerful opening in person or in print if you hope to have the opportunity to persuade. The best opening is one that creates immediate interest in what you have to say or induces intense curiosity.

The Zeigarnik Effect is attributed to Russian psychologist Bluma Zeigarnik. The Zeigarnik Effect says that people are more likely to remember things that are left incomplete than those that have been completed. This was first observed with waiters when it was noted that they remembered more of what was required by customers who had not paid their bills than those who had. The Zeigarnik Effect is also often referred to as the basis for the idea of cliffhangers in movies and books. Something is left incomplete, which creates tension that begs for closure, which keeps people watching. Howard Gossage was famous for using this technique in the 1960s, sometimes creating ads that just ended right in the middle of a thought. People had to know what came next. Internet marketer Mark Joyner was one of the first to repopularize the idea in direct marketing and persuasion.

The Zeigarnik Effect is a very powerful attention maintainer once you've gotten attention. By creating a cliffhanger, you leave people wanting to know more. They need closure and they stay with you as you implement your persuasion strategy.

Subliminal Selling Secret

When you are trying to persuade an individual or an audience, create tension by intentionally leaving something out. For example, give a list of three things that will make them successful with your product. Give them the first two ideas, each building up to a bigger and bigger crescendo with the

(continued)

> *(continued)*
> conclusion in number three. Before you give them number three, go into another piece of information. Allow the tension to build as they create an internal need for closure. Then give them number three, which will be a key idea that you want them to remember. Watch what happens to retention around the fulfillment piece; you'll be amazed.

SHORT AND SIMPLE

Every time I'm having difficulty getting a point across, it is because I violate this rule. Short sentences and simple words sell. If people need a literature professor or an Oxford English dictionary at hand to understand what you are saying, they won't be able to remember your point.

Simple words and short sentences are easy to digest. They make swallowing new ideas easy. Don't get me wrong, I'm a big advocate of extremely large vocabularies, but they are unnecessary in persuasion. I adore creating and reading an obtuse word salad, but it won't sell. Remember when we were talking about propaganda and covered sound bites? Sound bites are ideas reduced to their simplest form using the most understandable words.

Dennis Miller and Bill Maher are two of the funniest political comedians working today. I'm not sure there is another human being close to Dennis Miller as measured by the number of facts and references he has in his head. He also has one of the largest vocabularies I've ever heard. Guys like me find Dennis Miller hilarious, but many Americans don't, because they don't get his references or the subtlety in his language.

Bill Maher, love him or hate him, has an amazing grasp of facts and vocabulary as well. Bill is able to break ideas down into very simple sound bites that you can understand. Whether you agree with him or not, you get it. I'd love to see Bill Maher and Dennis Miller square off on a no-holds-barred pay-per-view debate. The verbal carnage and obtuse connections would be at epic proportions. Television would never be the same.

When you find resistance to persuasion, start looking at how the message is communicated. You'll nearly always find that there is confusion in the words and ideas that brevity and clarity will clear up.

Clarity and brevity equal belief.

TELL THEM WHAT YOU ARE GOING TO TELL THEM, TELL THEM, AND THEN TELL THEM WHAT YOU TOLD THEM

So the old adage goes. When it comes to subliminal persuasion and words, it is advice to heed. Consistency in your message makes it easier to understand. The more times someone hears something, the more they begin to believe it as long as it doesn't conflict with a deeply held belief. And, when it comes to changing beliefs, it just takes more time and more consistent messages with different levels of proof.

When you are developing arguments, it is often useful to have multiple setups that lead to the same conclusions. Those conclusions should be brief and easy to understand. When you present the argument in a number of different ways, the audience begins to feel that the core idea is familiar. Once they've heard many arguments, they will find one they agree with and accept.

Consistency also offers us great comfort. Use your words to create predictability to increase persuasion. You've probably had the experience of being able to finish someone else's sentence. Being able to draw a conclusion that completes your idea is a brilliant word strategy.

ASK THEM A QUESTION AND TELL THEM WHAT THEY WANT TO HEAR

One of the most overlooked persuasion tools is the use of powerful questions. Questions allow you to elicit the information that people need to hear to be persuaded. Once a question is answered, you simply have to craft a story that gives people the answer that they want to hear. Even when you have to present information that isn't the answer they want, you start by acknowledging what they want.

In the movie *Our Brand Is Crisis,* James Carville's political consulting firm is working on winning a presidential election in Bolivia. They poll nearly every day. The results of the polls become the basis for tomorrow's message. This strategy worked for them, as they generated a slightly over 1 percent victory, which is a win, but a very weak one. They went wrong because they didn't create big enough stories with enough consistency. Your stories must be easy to understand, consistent, and they must be self-fulfilling prophecies.

Vagaries in language allow you to let people fill in the blanks of their expectations. Being intentionally vague can often be beneficial as long as the audience fills in the blanks correctly. When people fill in the blanks, they need proof that they made the right decision. The defining step is to present them with what you know will occur as what they should expect.

The best way to understand what people need to hear is to ask very carefully crafted questions. Your questions must be directed at discovering the emotions, the processes behind the decisions that they make, and the beliefs that they hold. Questions that tend to get the most information are very specific open-ended questions. Here are a few examples:

- How do you know?
- Can you explain how ———— happens?
- How specifically does ———— occur?
- Has there ever been a time that ————?
- If you were going to explain ———— to someone, what would you say?
- Tell me about your experience with ————?
- How does ———— make you feel?
- How will you know when you've been successful with ————?

By asking open-ended questions that have a specific point in them, you get the information you need to feed back to them in your answers. When you are conducting mass persuasion, you need to feed the information back in a way that will allow people to hear what they need to hear but doesn't feel like they are being pandered to. Lip service is a persuasion killer. Ideally, when you present the information that they need to hear back to them, it is important that you allow some time to pass before you tell them.

There will be times, however, that you need to immediately tell them what they need to hear. There are two ways to handle it. One is to agree that whatever they need to hear exists.

The second way is to tell them what they need to hear in an example of you doing it for someone else. The third-party example doesn't feel like pandering and it demonstrates how it might work for them as well. For example, I might say to someone who has revealed that they need to get the approval of their spouse for a purchase. "A client yesterday explained to his spouse that buying and planting these trees added $10,000 in appraised value to their home and that really seemed to make sense to her. It is tough to say no to adding equity, isn't it?"

> **Subliminal Selling Secret**
>
> Begin your persuasion sequences by asking people to tell you what they need to hear. Ask them very powerfully engaging questions and listen carefully. Challenge what you hear to make sure you understand what you heard. I challenge by asking the question: "Does ———— mean ————?" or "What does that mean to you?"
>
> By asking that question, you get to the real explanation of what they mean by things that seem key. If they really are key, they'll explain themselves in a way that has some intensity or emphasis. They'll clarify for you. This is where you'll be paying particular attention, because this is often the information that you'll be spinning and giving back to them later.

PAINT BIG WORD PICTURES

The more vividly you describe something, the more likely people are to get pulled in to the explanation. Detail counts when you are building word pictures. You should focus on involving all the emotions possible. Let me paint a word picture of persuasion for you.

"You can tell when persuasion is occurring. First, you get a feeling of understanding that washes over you. Then just behind that comes that sense of surety that starts in the pit of your stomach. You can see the others around you as they get it, too, the understanding and excitement are nearly palatable. It feels exciting to get it. You feel compelled, moved forward as if on autopilot, to the action you must take. The voice in your head that normally questions your decisions is quickly quelled. You achieve a sense of peace, of determination. And, there is the anticipation of what is to come now that the decision has been made."

That is a large word picture. Allow me to show you another one.

"The skin on her right arm had the consistency of used sandpaper: cracked, worn out, and dried up from the sun."

These kinds of word pictures are easy to understand and for people to imagine. The subliminal persuader uses word pictures to cause people to imagine, because once they imagine, they enter the picture and become part of the experience themselves. They project the experience onto themselves, good or bad. If it is good, they want more; if bad, they want the solution. Your next word picture should walk them into the solution.

COVERT LANGUAGE

Before I start on this topic, I want you to understand I'm a big fan of neurolinguistic programming (NLP) and hypnosis as communication modalities. Used appropriately, they can have intensely effective results. Most people, however, pick and choose pieces from the modalities and don't understand how to use them. The result is that they often don't work and just end up sounding like bad language. Worse, people who hear you talk think they understand what you are doing and start telling you how much they admire your language patterns because of something they believe they heard.

Wow, it really feels good to get that off my chest. I'm not suggesting that you shouldn't study NLP or hypnotic language patterns. Quite the opposite, in fact. I'm suggesting that if you want to learn them, that you actually have to study them, and you should do it with a qualified trainer.

There is a lot of emphasis put on covert language in the persuasion community. You'll hear people talk about embedded commands, marked-out language or text, or hypnotic language structure. And while there is some validity to all of it, it is designed to be delivered when people are in a trance. It takes a very highly skilled linguist with a knowledge of hypnosis to make these kinds of techniques work. You don't learn them from a book; you learn them from face-to-face experiential training. You have to have someone show you what reactions you are looking for in people to understand whether you are being effective or not.

It sounds really cool to say that if you hide some words inside a sentence that people will take action based on it. Let me give you an example. Read the following sentence out loud.

By now, you may find yourself asking the question, "Will I take this now?"

Now, that sentence contains what some people would consider embedded commands. The first one is "By now." *By now* employs the idea of phonological ambiguity. A word that sounds the same as another in context is translated in context in the brain. So *By now* becomes *Buy now.* The next command is to "find yourself asking the question, 'Will I take this now?'" This is a combined command of telling you to ask yourself a question, then telling you to "take this now." Again, this could work in the right conditions, but most people are simply not skilled enough nor do they have enough time to properly condition the listener. The other problem with this kind of language and embedded commands is that in written form, people who don't know how to use this language won't read it properly in their head, so the impact is diminished.

A much better use of cover language is metaphor. The American Heritage Dictionary defines metaphor as "A figure of speech in which a word or phrase that ordinarily designates one thing is used to designate another, thus making an implicit comparison, as in *a sea of troubles* or *All the world's a stage* (Shakespeare)."

Your audience is able to interpret metaphor much more easily because they have experience not only interpreting, but creating, metaphor. Even when metaphors that have the same meaning are mixed, for example, "You reap what you sow and they will always come home to roost," your audience still understands what they mean.

Metaphor works because it allows you to take complex ideas and make them understandable by replacing the troublesome piece with something people already understand. They can make the connection. You should regularly use metaphor in all of your speaking and writing to become more persuasive. Metaphor is the fuel that combusts in the engine of persuasion.

Closely related to and often confused with metaphor is analogy. The definition of *analogy* at dictionary.com is "a similarity between like features of two things, on which a comparison may be based: *the analogy between the heart and a pump.*" When used properly, analogies are great clarifiers of ideas that may be hard to grasp.

When I was selling point-of-sale software that had integrated accounting, something that at the time was not common, I often used an analogy to make the connection for people. I'd say, "Integrated point-of-sale is like an ATM: You swipe your card, you get your money, your account is debited. When the customer makes a purchase, the point-of-sale software does the rest." The analogy was an easy way for them to get their head around how it might work based on a system they already understood and used.

Metaphor and analogy allow you to take the focus away from the technicalities of the language or the persuasion. They move the audience's focus to something they can understand and easily accept. Once they've accepted the metaphor or analogy, they are already agreeing, in most cases, with what comes next.

The covertness of the language is what is concealed by the analogy or the metaphor that slides in under the radar of critical analysis.

DEVELOPING EFFECTIVENESS WITH WORDS

You must constantly practice how you use words to become most effective with them. You must also pay particular attention to how other people use their words to influence as well.

Regardless of your political views, there have been some amazing communicators as presidents. The thing to pay attention to is how their words are combined. Most presidents don't write their own speeches; they are written by professional speechwriters. It is even better to observe and listen to the delivery and then read the words by themselves. My suggestion is that you carefully study the speeches of:

President John F. Kennedy
President Ronald Reagan
President Bill Clinton
Martin Luther King Jr.

These are some of the most profoundly effective persuaders of our time. When you understand how they use their words and overlay their model onto yours, your words will move into the background and your ideas will ignite the masses. That ignition of the people is the true essence of subliminal persuasion. It is where the seduction occurs.

Subliminal Selling Secret

Break apart one of your favorite speeches from one of the people in the earlier-mentioned list and practice delivering it until you can do it with the same intensity as the person who delivered it. Emulate their speaking style, their body language, and their eye movements. Practice their inflection and their intonation. Make it as precise as you can. Once you've mastered it, practice delivering your sales pitch in the same format. Emulate them completely, but make the words yours this time. This is true subliminal persuasion and leverages the power of someone who has mastered persuasion.

Language in persuasion is one of the least-understood subliminal persuasion tactics for several reasons. First, it is the area where people incorrectly assume proficiency exists; it doesn't. Proficiency in language comes from practice. The second reason that it is misunderstood is that proficiency takes a lot of practice. The more you practice your language, the better your skills will get. The better your skills get, the more people will be moved.

The more you study language and practice language in all forms, in writing and in person, the better you'll become at correctly identifying what people need to hear and be able to present it to them on a dime in any situation. But more important, you'll be able to deliver the information in a way that is simple and easy to understand, which leads to massive action.

Leverage your language. It is the most powerful tool you own.

Implementation Is Everything

Money Follows Action

Before you read the next chapter, take the following actions:.

- Develop a question set that you can use to extract the information that people need to hear so that you can build it into your persuasive strategy.
- Find the most complicated pieces of your presentation and see how you can use simpler ideas, better words, metaphors, or analogies to take the focus away from the complexity and increase understanding and acceptance.
- Identify the three best communicators in your field right now. Study them carefully, what they say, and how they say it.

Understand what makes them compelling. By doing a detailed analysis, you'll quickly understand exactly what you need to do to move the masses in your favor. You'll also find their weaknesses and those weaknesses that can be exploited to move the audience to your side.

ESSENTIAL FURTHER STUDY

Books

The Stuff of Thought—Steven Pinker (Viking, 2007)
Words That Work—Dr. Frank Luntz (Hyperion, 2007)

Movies

I Have A Dream—Martin Luther King Jr. (MPI Home Video, 2005)
Search YouTube and Google Video for clips of all presidents' major speeches.

Television

Choose at least one politician in whom you are interested and follow his speaking style. Listen to the words he uses, the way they're delivered, and the stories they tell.

10

CREATING A CULT FOLLOWING

Successful cult memes induce intense social interaction behavior between cult members.

— Author Keith Henson

I've been fascinated with the dynamics of cult followings, both destructive and benign, since I left the cult I grew up in. For companies and those who hope to develop growth most quickly and influentially, developing a cult following is a crucial undertaking.

Allow me to explain.

Cults are all about creating a community where like-minded people can share ideas and enthusiasm for those ideas or products. Let's look at some of the most successful business cults today:

- Scion
- Van's Shoes
- Jimmy Buffett Parrotheads
- Apple, Inc. (rapidly losing cult status)

- Harley Davidson
- Crocs Shoes
- Traeger Wood Pellet Barbecue Grills (growing cult status, but not of their own creation; it is consumer-developed)

Each of these companies has something in common. They have a highly dedicated group of people who are actively pursuing a lifestyle that the company or product promises. They find great emotional satisfaction from belonging and being a part of something bigger than themselves. These are not people who want to be perceived as different and alone. These people want to be perceived as being on the inside, part of something bigger than themselves that is fun and interesting. They want something that is different from their day-to-day reality that they can identify themselves with.

For many people, the groups they belong to are in some ways replacements for families that have become increasingly spread out and mobile. There is great comfort in being able to go someplace new and not be alone for long, because you can find a group that worships (I choose that word very intentionally) just like you do.

There are many obvious correlations between religion and cults. People join organizations to the extent that those organizations help them move closer and closer to self-actualization. They also gravitate to groups that actively recognize them. Go to Jimmy Buffett's web site (margaritaville.com) and see how much he interacts with his Parrotheads. Recognition builds connection, and connectedness creates evangelists who spread your message.

For the subliminal persuader, building a cult is essential, because your persuasion efforts can be directed at a much smaller group of people. Those brand cultists will then do the hard work of spreading your message. When I wrote my first book, I had to develop a following. When I released the second book, it reached the sales of the first book in about a third of the time. I suspect that this book will exceed both of those in an even shorter period of time because of the group of people who have come together around my ideas on persuasion. Those people will spread the word faster than I ever could through advertising, PR, or any other method. They'll spread it more profitably because they'll give the book their personal endorsement, which is worth everything when it comes to making a buying decision.

CONNECTEDNESS

One of the key reasons people join cults is to be part of a like-minded group. The most effective cult brands have a very formalized means for people to connect. They sometimes seed those efforts in the beginning, but they take on a life of their own as the groups grow.

People become part of a group because they are looking to have fun. They want to share their experiences using a product or service and they want to do it with like-minded individuals. This connectedness allows them to group and be different from the masses but have the support of others so that they don't feel alone.

> **Subliminal Selling Secret**
> Focus on building a following by creating a means for people to group. Harley did this effectively with their Harley Owners Group (HOG) and Apple did it with its Mac Users Group.
> *(continued)*

(continued)

Ask yourself how you can connect your users. Here are several ideas you can build on.

- Create an online group or forum
- Have an annual event that people can come to
- Create local or regional groups where like-minded people can connect. *Fast Company* magazine did this well with their Company of Friends. Just remember that there has to be an overriding theme that people are responding to, which has to evolve and remain interesting, or people will leave.

The real key to success is making sure that people have a venue for connecting with one another, not just with you. When you or a representative of the company connects in the groups, it should be a huge perk for the group; it should make them feel very special.

EXCLUSIVE ACCESS

Followers want exclusive access to things that the general public doesn't get. This level of access can be as simple as getting advance notice of certain things or can be as detailed as being invited into focus groups or design meetings. They need to feel like they are contributing to the myth, and when they do, they extend the myth.

IDENTITY

Followers are creating an identity for themselves based on the ideals that you or your product offers. It is very important that you build a powerful ideal with which they can connect.

Create a focus on showing people how to develop an identity that includes your ideals. Show them how that identity makes them better, more powerful, more complete. The more that they feel the identity is who they are, the more committed they will be in spreading your word.

Cult followings are the ultimate in subliminal persuasion because the members are visible and vocal. The information they share has the perception of being consumer generated (and often is). So, there is a natural perception that if everyone is doing it, then it must be the right thing to do. In many ways, cults are another form of social proof.

BUILDING THE CULT

Building a cult following is not as difficult as it seems at first, but it does take specific effort.

1. Create an ideal that is bigger than you and bigger than the product. Have a worldview that people can get behind. These ideas should also include an element of excitement and fun. Make them big ideas that don't feel too hard to carry out. The reason that many nonprofits have a hard time getting big followings is that their worldview, even if good, is too much work and there's not enough "feel good" to make it appealing.

2. Create your first event and make it very public to your users. Your event should honor and elevate your users as the real heroes of the event. Put it on your web site, talk about it in the media. Let people who weren't a part of it know what it was like and what they missed. Let them know how they can become a part of what you are doing

next. Encourage and support leadership that springs up from the group; help them help the group grow.

3. Educate your followers. Once the group starts to gain momentum, it is important to educate your followers. Give them more information about products, the company, and what is coming next. Share information about how others are using or benefiting from the product or service. Ask them to share their stories, make their stories key to the education of future members where appropriate.

4. Make it fun. Create more activities, events, and ideas that make being a part of the group fun. Show them more and more ways that their activity is actually living the lifestyle that you promote. The more engaged they become, the deeper their commitment.

5. Document their success. Have people take pictures, videos, and so on, of their gatherings or their uses of the product. Publicize those. Use social proof to make other people desirous of the experience that their peers are having.

6. Tell them what they should be experiencing. Give people clues about their success in embracing the ideals that you promote. Tell them how they'll know that they've been successful. Connect them with others who are true believers so that they can be further inculcated with the spirit of the worldview.

7. Give them a means of connecting to others. Show them how to get their friends involved. They should especially focus on people who are not already involved or even using the products, because they are valuable recruits. You can offer free product samples, trials, exclusive memberships based

on relationships, or any other number of inducements that can be offered by the followers to their friends.

8. Never stop praising them for their commitment. Be sure that you always acknowledge the value of the following you've created. By acknowledging their commitment and importance, you make them feel even more valued and a part of what you are all creating together.

LEADING YOUR CULT

One of the challenges of charismatic cult leaders is that they often experience terrible falls in front of their followers. When they fail, they become seen as being mere mortals. This is a real challenge for the narcissistic personality that leads destructive cults. It destroys a vital self-belief that they can rarely regain.

Fortunately, leading brand cultists is quite different. They don't rely as much on a centralized leader as they do a centralized idea or worldview. But even long after the person who was out front is gone, if the worldview was big enough, it will continue. Look at Elvis fans; his following is stronger now than it was before he died. I visited Graceland as part of my study into benign cults and saw people openly weeping and acting in reverence of being in Elvis's home. I also saw people lying on top of the grave in the yard and weeping tears of very real grief. When Jimmy Buffett stops performing, the idea of Margaritaville will not go away; the Parrotheads will carry it on profitably for all of Jimmy's successors. Those people will keep forwarding the worldview that is so important to them.

Leading those people is a very critical role that someone has to play. Once you begin developing a following, you must have a plan for how they will evolve. Left to their own devices, they may evolve in ways you wish they wouldn't, or worse, they lose interest.

It is critical to develop a visible spokesperson who embodies the ideas your followers are connecting with. It may be the CEO, but it often isn't; he may simply offer his support to the person who will lead the charge.

When you lead a group, cultists (or brand cultists) need to see the leader as the conduit to the source of their beliefs. That person should teach them, train them, reward them, and even occasionally scold them to get them to follow fully.

The plan that the leader lays out should include a consistent and frequent reminder of the worldview so that people remember what it was that they bought into. He should also always interject fun and excitement into the event and should be present at all major gatherings so that people get to touch and know him as a person.

There occasionally needs to be tension and a joint enemy. Introducing a threat to the sanctity of the group, and giving them something to fight for, makes the group more powerful. Be very careful with tension, though; don't introduce it just for the purpose of creating tension. On an ongoing basis, too much tension becomes tiresome. It is a balancing act to create just enough so that people feel committed to defending their belief, their way of life, and their products and services, but not so much that they just give up.

Leading the group also entails involving them at many levels. You should bring some trusted (read *carefully selected*) members of the group in for a higher level of interaction. You can do this through inviting them to focus groups or making them beta testers or giving them first access to a new product so they can share it with the rest of their group.

Always let your followers know about new releases, new services, or problems first. Address the faithful first and they'll help you with everyone else. Where it is practical and possible, it is a great idea to give your faithful advance purchase opportunities, discounts, or other incentives for being part of the group. Or, you can create a limited edition that is available only to them for their faithful service.

Work on building your cult following early and focus on it often. The more that people can identify with you and what you are doing, your beliefs, and your way of life, the further your ideas will spread and the more influence you will have.

If you want to see even more of this idea in action, visit subliminalpersuasionbook.com and click on the link that says "Join my cult." This is a total insiders' group and most people who haven't read this book will be frightened off by it, but it is the only way to learn some of the most powerful brand cult-development tactics that I teach and use. Don't worry, you are perfectly safe, but you'll be shocked by the information I share there.

Implementation Is Everything
Money Follows Action
Before you read the next chapter, take the following actions:.

- Carefully evaluate the people who are currently working with you or buying from you. Look at how you can create or leverage a worldview that you've already created to develop a rallying point. Once you've identified the rallying
(continued)

(continued)

point, write out a plan for introducing your worldview and the idea of an event around it to get followers engaged.

- Ask yourself how you can engage your current customers or followers in getting more involved in your organization. Can they help you on a design, give you feedback on a soon-to-be released product, or become a beta tester?
- Begin developing your leader. If it is you, build on your existing persona. If the leader is not you, carefully craft what the leader will look like, what the message will be, and how you'll disseminate the message.
- Ask yourself the question, "Can I set up a users' group, a social group, or an event around my product or service that will serve my following?"

ESSENTIAL FURTHER STUDY

Books

Prophetic Charisma—Len Oakes (Syracuse, 1997)

The Guru Papers—Joel Kramer and Diana Alstad (Frog Books, 1993)

Movies

Joseph Campbell and the Power of Myth (Mystic Fire Video, 2001)

11

SEDUCTION

Most virtue is a demand for greater seduction.
— Author Natalie Clifford Barney

I hope by now that you realize that this is not a book about persuasion at all; rather, it is about seducing your audience. Your goal as a persuader, as a mass influencer, is to make your audience desire you, to fall in love with you. To make them want more of you all the time.

Done properly, that is what persuasion does.

When persuasion doesn't work, like the quote at the beginning of this chapter, it is a demand for greater seduction.

True seductions take place over time. Little bits and pieces are revealed, tension is created, desire is heightened. Every interaction is over too soon and the next one takes too long. The intense longing, the heightened sense of awareness between moments, all build the fantasy.

Seduction works because of the desire to possess.

Over time, seduction breaks down the mental barriers, it penetrates the soul, and surrender is complete.

In that moment, the fantasy is complete.

So it goes with persuasion. Subliminal persuasion is really about seducing your audience, causing them to surrender and fall hopelessly in love.

When you begin to implement the subliminal persuasion tools that I've revealed in this book, you are seducing at the highest level. Whether you choose to use these techniques one on one or one on many, the objects of your desire will respond equally well.

When using these subliminal persuasion strategies, make your efforts pleasant, because that is what people respond to. When you build a cult following, remember that they have one overriding need, the need for salvation. They want to be served well, once and for all. They don't want to have to think about it again, they just want to be able to come back and be well served again.

Salvation and seduction have predictability in common. Predictability comes in the form of an experience that is the same with each engagement and intensifies with time. That is the guarantee that brings back the lover and the follower.

Implicit in salvation and seduction is an innate desire to protect from loss. No one wants to lose a potential lover or an experience they can count on. It is up to you to point out examples of what could happen, gently and subtly, as the relationship progresses, so your audience remembers to be thankful for their salvation and to continue to notice the ongoing seduction.

Subliminal Selling Secret

Seduction happens in layers. To increase your persuasive effectiveness, layer on the strategies in as many layers as possible. Approach your audience from as many different angles and media as possible to intensify the desire. Allow the audience to see others who've been successful, found their salvation, won the prize of seduction. Begin thinking about how you can become more gentle, more subtle, more consistent, and more visible to those you wish to persuade.

The great seducers of the world are effective because of their ability to create an intense desire with the smallest of moves, the subtlest of exposures, or the most carefully placed word. To that end, see how you can make your presentations, your pitch, and your offers seductive.

Then set out to seduce and never stop. Interest wanes when seduction stops. The seduction can and should change over time, but it should never stop.

Seductions set up long-term relationships when conducted appropriately with the right person. The same is true when seducing the masses. The real value from persuasion comes over time with a continued relationship. The real value is in repeat business.

All of your persuasive efforts should be directed at setting up long-term relationships that remain interesting and fun. The more that you can provide a sense of completeness and fulfillment for your audience, the longer they'll stay with you.

When others see someone being seduced, they want a part of the seduction for themselves. It is profitably important that

(continued)

(continued)

you allow as many people as possible to observe the seduction so that they are taken in as well. All of your efforts should be directed at exposing the seduction to the widest possible audience.

Your advertising should include visuals and graphics of the seduction. It should also include loving testimonials from those adoring fans who want to share their experience with everyone. A secret that no one ever tells marketers is that the prettiest ads don't sell; the most seductive ones do.

Remember that seduction is a story that someone is telling herself that you are supporting with your actions. The more that your efforts to influence her build on that story and make her desire you, the deeper the seduction. Your advertising must tell the story of what the audience truly desires, the thing that will leave them fully emotionally fulfilled, the idealized product that leads to perceived, if not real, self-actualization.

Advertising carries seduction to the receiver through the medium. It is important that your audience gets involved in the message and shares it with others who are important to them just as the lover has to share a love letter or a token. Advertising done well enhances the seduction faster than any other method, because delivery is predictable. The audience will get the message. But advertising doesn't cover all the possible places where the audience resides. It is a little like the seducer who winks once in a crowded room and hopes that the person he is trying to seduce was looking at him at the exact time he winked.

Be consistent in your advertising and the seduction will become sure. Test your seduction to be certain that you are sending the signals that appeal to the audience you are seducing.

One thing that seducers do better than nearly all persuaders is that they build in a feedback look, a test to see whether their efforts are having an impact. More money is wasted on hoping that the messages you are sending are seductive rather than actually testing and intensifying and testing again.

When your tests yield the most profitable results and your audience is responding, it is time to expand the seduction as widely as profitable. That means crossing media, testing new message delivery mechanisms, and continuing to test. It also means crossing into new audiences that haven't yet been swayed by your charm and charisma.

One question that always seems to arise when I'm training sales teams is, "Does seduction occur between members of the same sex?" The answer is nonsexual and the answer is yes. Men seduce men by creating desire for things like power, knowledge, money, and access. Men who find something compelling about other men are very likely to copy them or to desire to be more like them. (What man has not wanted to be like Indiana Jones or James Bond?) As hard as that is for some men to hear, the sooner you understand it, the more easily you can seduce them. For men, successful seduction shows up in the form of emulation. The same is true for women, of course. They say that imitation is the sincerest form of flattery. To me, it is the surest sign of a long-term relationship and profitability.

SOME FINAL THOUGHTS ON SEDUCTION

- Being a part of a group of like-minded people is seductive . . . being left on your own is not.
- Beliefs are seductive . . . dictates are not.

- Applied propaganda that appears as news, reviews, or media observations, is seductive . . . obvious PR is not.
- Visuals, textures, colors, photos, video clips, those are the bits of skin, the furtive glance that seduces . . . the hard sell message is not.
- Relationships, stories, hints, tips, and invitations are seductive . . . lists of features and benefits are not.
- Benevolence, concern, compassion, ease, access, beauty, is seductive . . . self-directed focus is not.
- Subliminal persuasion is seductive . . . manipulation is not.

It is my great hope that you'll use this book as a guide to all of your mass persuasion goals. If you apply this information on a regular basis, if you incorporate it in your sales efforts, your marketing efforts, and your advertising, you'll move the masses in ways no one in your industry will understand.

I look forward to hearing of your success. Drop me a note at info@boldapproach.com and let me know how you are using these strategies. Visit the blog on the web site and leave your comments and ideas.

You now possess knowledge that can transform your life and business forever. There is only thing left to do, and that is to take action.

Remember:

IMPLEMENTATION IS EVERYTHING

Money Follows Action

Be an Action Taker!

ESSENTIAL FURTHER STUDY

Books

The Art of Seduction—Robert Greene (Viking, 2001)

Movies

Visit squidoo.com/persuade to find interesting new persuasion videos that you can use

AFTERWORD

THE SCARIEST THING ABOUT SUBLIMINAL PERSUASION . . .

BEN MACK

Dear Dave,
The scariest thing about *your book* . . .

• There's no qualifier.

Here's the deal: Before I give one twenty-third of the persuasion secrets away that are given away in this book, I qualify my audience. Before I reveal my first true applicable tactic that people can begin implementing in their lives as they see fit . . . *I won't continue unless the audience agrees* that every human on Earth deserves drinkable water. If anybody objects, I want to uncover their values quickly because these tools are too powerful for the masses.

And that is what makes your book dangerous.

There's no qualifier on this book. *Anybody can pick it up and instantly learn these skills.* This is a how-to manual to get whatever you want, provided you are willing to give up your preconceived notions about how things must be and accept how people are.

Most people will never comprehend the power of subliminal persuasion. They live in ignorant bliss that what they can't see won't hurt them. This secret knowledge is usually abused to start cults or control the masses, but, Dave, you are explaining not just how it works but how to do it.

You have gone too far.

Anybody who can't see the value of pushing the buttons of human action and emotion won't see the value of this book, either. Advertising that looks like advertising is third-rate propaganda. What we don't see influencing us is the most powerful form of persuasion.

You've revealed exactly how to move persuasion to the background while seducing the masses.

Let me put it another way. Which has a greater impact on whether or not you purchase from Banana Republic:

A. Banana Republic ads, or . . .

B. Whether the employees make you feel welcomed?

If you are like most people, the correct answer is B.

You know that much of what employees are supposed to say to you is scripted. You know that teams of people get paid big bucks to engineer a more profitable shopping experience for you to enjoy. You noticed during Bush's second inauguration that the limousines had Cadillac emblems on their grills. You get that these are actually tanks in the shape of limousines. You could launch a rocket at any of those so-called limos and they would bounce off and the passengers would survive. So you are left pondering how did Cadillac get its emblem on these grills that just happened to be on *every television network* in the United States. You can see the product placement.

Seeing it is one thing, and recognizing it is there is one thing, but you dare to teach the average business owner how to do it. It is empowering, and it is dangerous, because it challenges the decades-long death grip that corporations and politics have had on true persuasion.

I get that the readers of any of your books are smarter than the average bear. However, Dave, you went too far. *Subliminal Persuasion* is too good of a teacher. There is a difference between educating the masses so they can defend themselves, and arming the tyrants. That's what you've done. You have given the tools of mass control to whoever seeks out a book like this, which includes a lot of very sick minds.

Are you comfortable with that?

It is irresponsible to teach these tactics, to teach this material, and make these ideas so accessible.

With guarded respect,

Ben

think=>Dr. Ben Mack

Author of *Think Two Products Ahead* (Wiley, 2007)

P.S. For those readers who fear my assessment was too hard on Dave and *Subliminal Persuasion,* allow me to tell you what I learned from this book that is so valuable to me personally . . . and I hope will be to you as well.

In what other mass-distributed book have you read about the greatest marketer of the twentieth century, Edward Bernays? None that I have found, and certainly not with Dave's candor, and I've looked. Seriously, I'm a Google Ninja and I comb all sorts of bookstores and this is the most straight-up coverage on the invisible college of understanding mass influence and mind control techniques.

When I find knowledge like I discovered in this book, I call it seeing the zeros, seeing what's going unspoken, unwritten, and only reported in small circles of practitioners and the occasional confessional of a reformed economic hitman, but rarely in the mainstream press. That is what scares me about this book and why my chastisement.

Thank you, Dave, for helping me better understand the nuances of Subliminal Persuasion that I hadn't seen before. It truly is valuable to me and I'm certain to everyone who reads this book. My hope is that sociopaths don't spend a lot of time in the business section.

The question I hear you asked most often is: "How do you know so much about persuasion?" and you reply, "When you are fascinated by the subject like I am, you study deep and wide. You study the weird connections, the offshoots, the experts, and the oddballs. What I share here just scratches the surface of my breadth of knowledge, but it is the most important knowledge, that knowledge that turns a beginner into an expert and an expert into a master." Thank you for sharing with so many in a friendly way. A book like this is a primer, a synthesis, a catalog, almost, of where people can get more and similar information. And, you cracked the code on getting this information through traditional distribution. Your editor, Matt Holt, is a brave man.

Dave, you have amazed me again, and again, and again. Just when I believe that I've read every seminal book on advertising, you send me the *Book of Gossage* as a gift and I see a large hole in my education. You show me my zeros, where there could be knowledge and there isn't. Thank you for giving so much to me in so many ways. I hope my sharp criticism, which is meant with all respect, won't damage our friendship. I often worry for a humanity that doesn't worry enough for itself and is often led astray. The information in this book gives those who would use it for their unethical gain everything they need to know to create a cult. I also see where it helps the legitimate businessman create a fad.

The neat part of you showering me with zeros, where I see gaps in my knowledge, is that as you show me more and more zeros in my perception, I keep seeing more and more zeros in my bank accounts. . . . I mean zeros with commas. This is truly valuable information. The more I see how persuasion works, the more I see how to increase my effectiveness and get more money, get yeses faster, and have more time for myself.

By avoiding unwanted influence, I waste less time, have more time for myself and my family, and have so much less stress in my life.

That's the greatest gift on this planet—time. Your effectiveness training has given me my life back. Controlled time is our true wealth.

With sincere gratitude I remain,

Your friend,
Ben

APPENDIX

COACHING FOR INFLUENCE

DR. RACHNA D. JAIN

Coaching is one of the most significant methods for gaining influence over others. While usual discussions of coaching focus on the "helping others" aspect, which is, of course, important, little focus has been given to the concept of coaching for influence.

The interest in coaching has been rising over the past five years, and coaching is being hailed as one of the hottest human service fields. This growth is expected to continue as more corporations are employing coaches to boost employee productivity and results. There are coaches for everything: relationships, business, writing, peak performance, wellness, and fitness; you name it, there is someone who coaches it.

Though you have likely heard of coaching, I don't expect you'll have heard of it treated in the way we cover it here.

Appropriate for a book on subliminal persuasion, coaching is a form of subliminal persuasion and one that nobody wants you to know.

Consider it this way: As a coach, you have ethically and directly moved yourself into a position of influence over your clients. They are, essentially, seeking your advice and guidance because they want to change their behavior or have a strong desire to believe that their life experience could be improved from what it is today.

Dave Lakhani's book, *Persuasion: The Art of Getting What You Want,* identifies three necessary preconditions for effective persuasion: motivation, participation, and reward. Coaching clients are motivated to interact; this is demonstrated by them seeking out coaching in the first place, or they are motivated to interact because it is a requirement for their job. Either way, they are motivated. Coaching demands huge participation, as the client is called upon to behave differently, going toward the changes he wants to make. Reward comes from changes in the self-concept and resulting feedback from the environment. Combined, the coaching relationship is a fertile place for persuasion.

While all coaches must be ethical and have integrity, it is also important that coaches be comfortable with the amount of influence they have over their clients. I have been coaching and consulting for more than eight years, and I know, undoubtedly, that I have (and continue to have) influence over all the clients I've ever worked with—even years later.

How do I know?

I know from the e-mails they send me, the acknowledgments they give me, and how their lives are changed from our work together. It's very common for me to receive e-mails from clients with whom I haven't spoken in years and they refer to a recent life event and explain, "I took action because I could hear you in my head saying I should do this."

In psychology, this is referred to as *introjection,* where the patient has absorbed the qualities of the therapist to further support the patient's self-concept. Another way of thinking about introjection is as a form of persuasion. When a client has introjected your message, it means that she is continually influenced by it. What would that kind of influence mean for your business? Imagine if you could have this kind of influence over your clients, years and years later? How would it be if they e-mailed you and said, "I just knew I needed to take this action because I heard you in my head, telling me it was a good idea?"

Introjection also occurs in coaching, as the client begins to embody the traits and qualities of the coach. If the client has come to coaching to improve time management, presumably the coach is an expert on time management. If the coaching is effective, the client gradually adopts new behaviors under the guidance and direction of the coach. (Sounds like persuasion, doesn't it?)

As a coach, you are in a position of authority and *gurudom* over your clients. The clients have sought you out because you are an expert and well-known in your field. They are naturally predisposed to follow what you say, especially when they have the additional motivation to get their money's worth from working with you.

As I've stated previously, all coaches must be ethical and have integrity. They must be outcome-focused and goal- and time-oriented. This means they treat their clients respectfully and honestly, while being on track to guiding the client to a particular outcome in a certain amount of time. The focus on ethicality, outcome, and goal achievement are the basic foundations of persuasion. You cannot persuade in the long term if you do not focus on these factors throughout the relationship.

Another element of the coaching relationship is accountability, which refers to making mutual commitments and meeting them. This is a key component of the coaching relationship, which is based on accountability, support, and structure. The coach provides a framework for the client to change, and then supports and guides the change process.

During a period of change, it is expected that the client will adopt new beliefs and new ways of thinking. The coach acts as a mentor to help smooth these changes so they are less jarring. The coach functions as a sounding board for the client, identifying key patterns and behaviors that are supporting the change, and those that are hampering the change.

Coaches will often use humor to deepen the relationship. They are often likable and worth emulating. Their persona is one that supports their professional identity. They will often share appropriate stories about themselves and their own lives, which functions to increase the level of empathy clients feel, leading to even more influence with these clients.

The most effective coaches are actively influencing their clients, all the time. While the standard line about coaching is that "The Client leads, the Coach follows," this is not truly the case. If the client were leading the coaching sessions, very little would happen. The sessions would be focused on the client swirling around in his thoughts and processes, the very same ones he came to coaching to change. A better analogy is that the coach is driving the sessions, and the client points out scenic turns and probable rest stops along the way.

This is an important distinction, because you must be willing to exert influence if you are going to coach others. You must be comfortable accepting a certain level of responsibility for this other person's life, and find a way to be directive, guiding, and supportive, all at the same time.

Conversely, if you want to gain greater influence over others, offer to coach them in your processes and methods. Every business does something very well. These areas of strength are the very ones that should be turned into a coaching program for your clients.

Remember, your clients are often struggling with the very same issues you have. They have concerns about sales, marketing, budgets, and finding good employees. If you have a process or method that would improve your customer's business, you have an obligation to share your process with customers who would be interested.

While your product may be widget X, you can move your company into a position of influence with your clients by coaching them on how to get the most value from widget X. Offer training on using widget X to achieve goal Y. Guide them in how to use and benefit from your product or service, and they will purchase more of it.

If you want to influence, you must have opinions, and share them. If one brand of product is inferior, and your client is considering purchasing that brand, share your opinion. Give your client the full facts necessary to make a good decision.

One of the best ways to retain clients for the long term is to position yourself not as a provider of a service or product, but as a coach, mentor, and adviser for life. This elevates you from the realm of being a commodity, just like every other service or product provider out there, to an exalted status, where you have the best interests of your customer in mind and at heart. As a trusted adviser and coach, you will help the client make good decisions, which, naturally, will include considerations of your product or service as well.

To position yourself as a coach or adviser, you must be willing to be creative. Find new uses for your product or service, and share these with your customers. Provide structure, guidance, and feedback where appropriate. Follow up once every few months and make sure your product or service is still meeting their needs. Provide them with good information and recommendations for ancillary products or services. Connect them with your preferred resources. Make referrals.

When you make the shift toward trusted adviser, you have the opportunity to know your clients more deeply and interact with them more personally. The more you know your clients and the more deeply you interact with them, the greater your level of influence over them. The more you demonstrate that you care about them, as people, the more willing they will be to do business with you, and to refer their family, friends, and associates.

Coaching is a powerful process. It taps into the needs we all have for growth, improvement, and expansion, and that goes both ways. Coaching changes clients, and coaching changes coaches.

Remember, all business is about relationships. Using a coaching framework for interaction is an effective and persuasive method for building relationships. If you enter every professional conversation looking to coach the listener to his own best outcome, your conversations will be powerful, meaningful, and potentially life-changing. By using tools such as deep listening, asking questions, using curiosity, and empathy, you will be moving yourself into a position of influence within the conversation. Offering appropriate recommendations will further cement your position of influence—and these recommendations can be just about anything. If you are talking about baseball, you can make a recommendation about baseball. If you are talking about movies, you can make a recommendation about movies.

By giving a solid recommendation about any relevant aspect of the conversation, you have begun the process of positioning yourself as a trusted adviser. Not that all of your client conversations should be about baseball or movies (unless these are your business areas, of course), but the idea is that good recommendations and communication in one area can carry over into others. This means that if clients see you as a resource in one area, they will be more likely to search for ways in which you can be a resource in other areas, as well.

We all are looking for a place to belong, a community, and a warm place to call *home*. Using these coaching-for-influence strategies will help you gather a group of your own people—those who value and appreciate the same things as you, and, who also just happen to be customers of your business. When you can create this feeling of warmth, support, and home, you have turned your occasional customers into raving fans.

As I've said, all businesses can add a coaching component. It may take some thought about how and what you would coach your clients on, but adopting a coaching stance will move you into a position of influence with your clients. And more influence means more money.

One of the biggest complaints of coaching programs is that they are time-intensive and resource-heavy. This need not be the case. There are several methods for developing an effective and profitable coaching program for online use. The outcome of these programs is to present your clients with directed learning activities, feedback, structure, and a chance to practice new behaviors.

There are many poorly designed coaching programs out there. These lead to customer frustration and dissatisfaction, which can ruin your company's prospects and brand.

On the other hand, adding a well-designed and well-implemented coaching component to your marketing and sales process can have huge benefits. A helpful and focused program will result in happier customers and higher profits. Your customers will feel that you truly care about them, refund requests will diminish, and your customers will refer others to you.

Given these benefits, it's not the question of whether you can afford to add a coaching program. The question is: Can you afford not to?

For more information, contact Dr. Rachna Jain at:

TheCoachCreator.com

11700 Montgomery Road

Beltsville, MD 20705

coach@TheCoachCreator.com

BIBLIOGRAPHY

Barkow, Jerome, Leda Cosmides, and John Tooby. *The Adapted Mind: Evolutionary Psychology and the Generation of Culture.* New York: Oxford University Press, USA, 1992.

Bell, Catherine. *Ritual Theory Ritual Practice.* New York: Oxford University Press, USA, 1992.

Bloom, Howard. *The Lucifer Principle: A Scientific Expedition into the Forces of History.* New York: Atlantic Monthly Press, 1997.

Cialdini, Robert. *The Psychology of Influence.* New York: HarperCollins, 2006.

Conway, Flo, and Jim Siegelman. *Snapping: America's Epidemic of Sudden Personality Change.* New York: Stillpoint Press, 1995.

Damasio, Antonio. *The Feeling of What Happens: Body and Emotion in the Making of Consciousness.* San Diego: Harvest Books, 2000.

Dawkins, Richard. *The God Delusion.* Boston: Houghton Mifflin, 2006.

Dawkins, Richard. *The Selfish Gene.* New York: Oxford University Press, USA, 2006.

Dillard, James Price, and Michael Pfau. *The Persuasion Handbook: Developments in Theory and Practice.* Thousand Oaks, CA: Sage Publications, Inc., 2002.

Green, Robert. *The Art of Seduction.* New York: Penguin, 2003.

Green, Robert. *The 33 Strategies of War.* New York: Viking Adult, 2006.

Green, Robert. *The 48 Laws of Power.* New York: Penguin, 2000.

Goldman, Daniel. *Social Intelligence: The New Science of Human Relationships.* New York: Bantam, 2007.

Hawkins, David R. *Power vs. Force: The Hidden Determinants of Human Behavior.* Carlsbad, CA: Hay House, 2002.

Heinrichs, Jay. *Thank You for Arguing: What Aristotle, Lincoln, and Homer Simpson Can Teach Us About the Art of Persuasion.* New York: Three Rivers Press, 2007.

Hogan, Kevin. *Covert Persuasion: Psychological Tactics and Tricks to Win the Game.* Hoboken, NJ: John Wiley & Sons, 2006.

Hogan, Kevin. *The Psychology of Persuasion: How to Persuade Others to Your Way of Thinking.* Gretna, LA: Pelican Publishing Company, 1996.

Kilbourne, Jean. *Can't Buy Me Love: How Advertising Changes the Way We Think and Feel.* New York: Free Press, 2000.

Kramer, Joel, and Diana Alstad. *The Guru Papers: Masks of Authoritarian Power.* Berkeley, CA: Frog Books, 1993.

Laermer, Richard, and Mark Simmons. *Punk Marketing: Get Off Your Ass and Join the Revolution.* New York: HarperCollins, 2007.

Luntz, Dr.Frank. *Words That Work: It's Not What You Say, It's What People Hear.* New York: Hyperion, 2007.

Packard, Vance. *The Hidden Persuaders.* New York: Pocket, 1984.

Paul, John, and Deborah Micek. *Secrets of Online Persuasion: Captivating the Hearts, Minds and Pocketbooks of Thousands Using Blogs, Podcasts and Other New Media Marketing Tools.* Garden City, NY: Morgan James Publishing, 2006.

Pinker, Steven. *The Stuff of Thought: Language as a Window into Human Nature.* New York: Viking Adult, 2007.

Rapaille, Clotaire. *The Culture Code: An Ingenious Way to Understand Why People Around the World Live and Buy as They Do.* New York: Broadway Books, 2007.

Rushkoff, Douglas. *Coercion: Why We Listen to What "They" Say.* New York: Riverhead Trade, 2000.

Sargant, William. *Battle for the Mind: A Physiology of Conversion and Brainwashing.* Cambridge, MA: Malor Books, 1997.

Sosnik, Douglas B., and Matthew J. Dowd and Ron Fournier. *Applebee's America: How Successful Political, Business, and Religious Leaders Connect with the New American Community.* New York: Simon & Schuster, 2007.

Surowiecki, James. *The Wisdom of Crowds.* New York: Anchor Books, 2005.

Underhill, Paco. *Why We Buy: The Science of Shopping.* New York: Texere Publishing, 2001.

Williams, Roy. *The Wizard of Ads: Turning Words into Magic and Dreamers into Millionaires.* Austin, TX: Bard Press, 1998.

Winn, Denise. *The Manipulated Mind: Brainwashing, Conditioning and Indoctrination.* Cambridge, MA: Malor Books, 2000.

- Zaltman, Gerald. *How Customers Think: Essential Insights into the Mind of the Market.* Boston: Harvard Business School Press, 2003.
- Zinsser, William. *On Writing Well, 30th Anniversary Edition: The Classic Guide to Writing Nonfiction.* New York: HarperCollins, 2006.

About the Author

Dave Lakhani is the world's first Business Acceleration Strategist and president of Bold Approach, Inc., a business acceleration strategy firm helping companies worldwide immediately increase their revenue through effective sales, marketing, and public relations.

Considered one of the world's top experts on the application of persuasion and Applied Propaganda, Dave's talks are in high demand and heard by corporations and trade organizations of all sizes worldwide. His advice is regularly seen in *Selling Power* magazine, *Sales and Marketing Management*, the *Wall Street Journal*, *Investor's Business Daily*, *INC.*, *Entrepreneur*, the "Today" show, and hundreds of other media outlets. Dave is also the host of "Making Marketing Work," a radio talk show focused on marketing strategy for growing businesses. Dave also authored *Persuasion: The Art of Getting What You Want* (Wiley, 2005), *The Power of an Hour* (Wiley, 2006), *A Fighting Chance* (Prince Publishing, 1991), a section of the anthology *Ready, Aim, Hire* (Persysco, 1992), and the audiobook *Making Marketing Work* (BA Books, 2004).

Dave has owned more than 10 successful businesses in the last 20 years and considers himself a serial entrepreneur and committed business builder. An avid student and life-long learner, Dave has studied every major sales, marketing, or influence professional in the past 20 years. He's a Master Practitioner of Neurolinguistic Programming (NLP) who has studied with NLP's founder, Richard Bandler, and is a graduate and former adjunct faculty member of The Wizard of Ads Academy.

Dave lives in Boise, Idaho, with his wife, Stephanie, and his daughter, Austria. When not on the road with clients or speaking, Dave enjoys scuba diving, skiing, martial arts, reading, and great wine.

Visit Dave online at www.subliminalpersuasionbook.com or boldapproach.com.

INDEX

webvideouniversity.com
infomercial toolkit